God Has A REASON
for EVERYTHING

God Has A
REASON
—for—
EVERYTHING

A Book of Tragedy and Miracles
That Can Make You Believe
There is No Such Thing as a Coincidence

CHERY MANNING

New York

God Has A REASON *for* EVERYTHING
A Book of Tragedy and Miracles That Can Make You Believe There is No Such Thing as a Coincidence

Published in New York, New York, by Morgan James Publishing. Morgan James and The Entrepreneurial Publisher are trademarks of Morgan James, LLC. www.MorganJamesPublishing.com

The Morgan James Speakers Group can bring authors to your live event. For more information or to book an event visit The Morgan James Speakers Group at www.TheMorganJamesSpeakersGroup.com.

ISBN 978-1-63047-694-6 paperback
ISBN 978-1-63047-695-3 eBook
Library of Congress Control Number:
2015911001

Cover Concept Art Donated by:
Linda Baldigo

Cover Design by:
Rachel Lopez
www.r2cdesign.com

Interior Design by:
Bonnie Bushman
The Whole Caboodle Graphic Design

In an effort to support local communities and raise awareness and funds, Morgan James Publishing donates a percentage of all book sales for the life of each book to Habitat for Humanity Peninsula and Greater Williamsburg.

Get involved today, visit
www.MorganJamesBuilds.com

Habitat
for Humanity®
Peninsula and
Greater Williamsburg
Building Partner

*This book is dedicated to the memory of
Jason Keith Robbe, with all the love and support
from my family and friends.*

Contents

Acknowledgments

This story would not be complete without the help of my family, the Robbe family, and Jason's best friend, Joe. I have compiled information through these people that I wouldn't have any other way. The coma took a good three weeks away from my life that I still don't remember. Thank you for all your time and effort to provide me with this information in the timely manner you did.

CHAPTER 1

My History

S he's *flat-lining! Get the paddles! HURRY!" yelled the pilot. They pulled out the portable unit and quickly placed the pads on me and grabbed the paddles.*

"CLEAR!" he yelled, as he sent electric shock through my body to try to revive my heart. Everyone pulled away from me as the shockwave went through my entire body, lifting me up off the ground for only a split second. Nothing!

"Hit her again!" he said, as they pumped up the machine again. "CLEAR!" This time, they got a heartbeat. "Okay, we've got her back. Let's get her in the chopper and head out," yelled the pilot. They got everything packed up, loaded me into the chopper, and we were off to the hospital.

On the way to the hospital, I flat-lined again. They were able to get me back one more time. They knew there wasn't much time left for me.

After the explanation of that day, I remember thinking to myself, "Every girl I've ever known has had a dream they wish to have fulfilled

1

when they get older—a man who fits every aspect of what they would like their husband to be. When you finally find that man, you never think of anything that can separate you. Then, when you least expect it, it happens."

//////////////////////////

Since I was seven, my dream was to be a movie scriptwriter. When I graduated high school, I wanted to move to California and study filmmaking. I had written my first full movie script in the eighth grade, during study hall class. It was called "After the Empire." I am a huge *Star Wars* fan and wanted so much to write this script with George Lucas. What can you expect? I was only thirteen years old. I sent separate copies to 20th Century Fox Films, George Lucas, Harrison Ford, and Mark Hamill. I got all the copies back, with a letter from 20th Century stating how impressed they were with my enthusiasm about *Star Wars*, but that they couldn't read the scripts anyone sends in, due to policy. They also reminded me that *Star Wars* was copyrighted and that I could not use it.

I was upset, of course, but more determined than ever to get my own story out there. I didn't tell them how old I was. They gave me the address for the Screen Writers Guild so I could join and keep writing. Unfortunately, you had to be eighteen to join, another push backward for me.

I did start to write my own story. I still have never seen it out as a movie.

Now, that doesn't mean that it's not already out there or something close to it anyway. I haven't seen every movie ever made. That would cost too much money. I can't even say what it's about at this point, just because if I do get it out there, then the story is already known and not so interesting.

I was the typical teenager. I had lots of crushes on different people growing up. I think my first crush was on Ricky Schroeder from *Silver Spoons*. Then it went to Ralph Macchio, after I saw *The Karate Kid* when I simply had to join a martial arts class. My junior year in high school, *Top Gun* came out and I fell in love with Tom Cruise. I would follow him for a long time until he did *Interview with a Vampire*. Things kind of changed for me after that. In high school, my boyfriend and I watched *Top Gun*, *The Color of Money*, and *Cocktail*. I had no idea how much impact these movies would have on us later in life. Our relationship, however, didn't last.

My mother was totally against me moving to LA. She said, "There's no way I'm letting my eighteen-year-old daughter from Wasilla, Alaska, move to Los Angeles. They'll eat you alive. You have no relatives there and you will be totally on your own."

My mother suggested my older sister, Dawn, and I go to the DeVry School of Technology in Phoenix. We had relatives there and it wouldn't be such a bad place to live. After many discussions, my sister and I headed for Phoenix. My mother had the mind-set of, since we're moving into the computer age, maybe we should go to school for business management or computer programming or something. At least that way, we'd always be able to find a job.

We ended up in Phoenix, in October of 1988. The next semester started on Halloween. Dawn and I had spent some time looking for just the right place to rent an apartment. We found the perfect place on Nineteenth Avenue and Thunderbird. We lived just across the street from some very big-named celebrities, even though we never saw any of them. It was always fun to let everyone know who our neighbors were, like Stevie Nicks.

After starting school, the first trimester was pretty standard. Classes were just to get an idea of how much you really knew. The first trimester was for getting to know people and settling in, from what I could tell. There were lots of parties and functions where you could interact with your classmates. Things had started to change when I started into my second trimester.

Dawn and I realized that we needed to find jobs to keep us going. We had saved money from jobs during the summer, but it wasn't going to last long. We both took jobs at Burger King, on the corner of our street. We had experience since we worked in one back home in Wasilla in the summer of 1986. We were hired within a week from arriving in Phoenix. It was looking good so far.

When we started our jobs, I was placed in the front to take orders. Dawn was in the back making burgers, which didn't make sense to us. We had worked the exact opposite back home. I made all the burgers and she worked the front. It was like learning a whole new job. After the first night of work, Dawn decided to quit. She said she saw roaches in the back and couldn't deal with that. They refused to put her out in front with me. I went back to work for two more days, then I also quit after my shift. Things were not looking so good at this point. Nothing else was available in our area and we didn't have a car either. Luckily, we had a Safeway on the corner of Nineteenth and Thunderbird that was within walking distance. We spent as little as we could when buying food. The typical college food was mac-n-cheese, Top Ramen and spaghetti. Fruit was quite inexpensive there, compared to what we were paying back in Alaska, so we bought it as well. The walks were occasionally accompanied by a shopping cart, which would eventually make its way back to the store on the next trip.

On Christmas vacation, I had gone home to Alaska and run into my old high school sweetheart. Bruce had been introduced to someone else the night before I left for Arizona who he was dating now. He was supposed to spend the evening with me, the night before I left and was about two hours late. When he finally arrived, I smelled perfume on him, but was just glad to see him. I didn't say anything about the perfume until I found out later what had happened. I wasn't too wild about men after that. I swore men off and wasn't going to even think about another man for quite awhile.

CHAPTER 2

We Met

When I got back to school in January, we started to look on the work board at DeVry. There were businesses that hired students all the time. We thought one sounded pretty good and the hours were perfect for school. We set up appointments to get interviews and crossed our fingers. I was interviewed and hired by MCI Telecommunications as a part-time telemarketer. Then Dawn got hired about one week later by a different supervisor. Our scheduled hours were from 4:30 to 9pm Monday through Friday.

They weren't supposed to hire relatives for the same department. No one had any idea that we were even related, at first. We looked a lot different from each other. All they knew was that we lived together and went to the same school.

Since we had no transportation, we always took the bus where we needed to go. I had never gotten a driver's license. There always had been someone to drive me around. Dawn did have a driver's license, but no car at first, and was a little nervous about taking the test in such a big city. That eventually changed.

While we were at work, we started talking to people that we worked with to see if there was anyone else who lived close to us who could give us rides to work each day. Dawn found someone who lived in the same complex we did and it worked out great. Her name was Lynette. She lived with her friend, Robby, in the next building over from us.

One day, about three weeks after working at MCI, Dawn was going to do something with Lynette after work. I was set up to ride home with someone else. I wasn't told who it was, just that he'd be waiting in the lobby after work, at the elevators.

After my shift was over, I headed down in the elevator, unsure of what to expect. When the doors opened, I saw him standing there. I was so nervous. He was gorgeous! He had short dark hair, neatly combed back, brown eyes, a very fit and stocky stature, and was just a little shorter than me. He was carrying a briefcase. His smile just made you want to melt. He was wearing a very shiny, silky dark gray shirt with dark dress pants and a tie. The pants and shirt were creased in all the right places. He introduced himself, "Hi, I'm Jason Robbe," as he put out his hand to shake mine.

"Hi, I'm Chery. Are you the one who's going to drive me home tonight?" I asked.

"Yes. If you're okay with that," he replied with a big smile.

"Do you know how far out I live?" I asked, hoping that it wouldn't be a problem.

"Yes, I do. You live very close to me." He smiled again, and then continued. "I live right off Thunderbird where the Circle K is at. Do you know where that is?"

Me and Jason standing by tree

He had a curious look on his face. "I know you just moved here and I don't know how much you've seen."

I smiled at him, "Yes, I think I've walked there a couple of times. I know it's just off the highway, right?"

"Yes. They just finished filming a movie there. It's called *Bill and Ted's Excellent Adventure*. They also filmed it at the Metro Center." He had an excited look on his face as well. "Have you been there yet?" We started to head for the main entrance.

"Yes, but only for short periods of time. I can't shop a lot because I have to take everything home on the bus. My sister and I don't have a car yet, as you already know," I said with a smile.

We walked out of the MCI building and went toward the parking garage. I was stepping down the stairs when a very large sewer roach ran right across the sidewalk in front of me. I stopped with a very surprised, confused, and nervous look on my face. I stared at the ground and pointed, "Is that what I think it is?" I asked, not really sure if I wanted to hear the answer to the question.

"Yes. It's a sewer cockroach. They get very big here in the downtown area. Be careful, because they aren't afraid of you either. I've had them chase me down in the garage," he said. With that comment, I made it to his car as fast as I could.

What a car! It was a 1989 Honda Prelude, cherry red with detailed work. The wheels had inky directional rims colored to match the car, four-wheel steering, and a fin in the back. It also had a sunroof and had the word Prelude down both sides of the car. From the front, it looked like a Ferrari. Everything on the inside was automatic.

Jason standing next to his car

"WOW! Nice car!" I said.

"Thanks. I just got it," he said very excitedly. "I've been saving up for a while. I wanted to make sure I could get all that I wanted in it."

He power unlocked the doors and opened my side. "Get in."

"Thank you," I said. The inside was immaculate! Black, plush seats with a black interior and wood trim highlights. The car smelled like his cologne.

"You're welcome," he replied. He shut the door behind me. He walked around the backside of the car, opened the passenger door on the driver's side, and placed his briefcase in the backseat. He then proceeded to get in the driver's seat next to me and started the car.

"Is that your cologne that I smell?" I asked.

"Yes, it's Obsession. It smells better than the new car smell, so I use it in here as well," he said with a smile. "Is it too overwhelming for you? I can roll the window down a bit, if you want me to."

Without hesitation and being pleasantly surprised, I answered, "No, I think it smells very nice. I've never known anyone who uses cologne as an air freshener in the car. That's a great idea!"

The whole time, I'm thinking, "Could this really be happening to me? Could I really have just met someone, out of my league, who seems truly interested in talking with me? So much for swearing off men."

We talked the entire way home. It was about a half hour drive. We had a lot in common and had a very exciting conversation. He told me about all the girls at work who wanted to date him. At that point, my hopes for him asking me out started to plummet. I began to think that I was going to be just another number to call. I was happy to have had a good conversation with him.

When he pulled up to the complex where my apartment was, I didn't want to get out of the car. We continued our conversation for at least another half hour.

"Well, I better let you get home. It's late and we both do have to work tomorrow as well," I said. "Thank you for the ride home. It was very nice getting to know you. I hope we can do this again."

"I'm sure we can arrange that, if you want. How about, I pick you up for work tomorrow and we can continue our conversation then?" he asked.

I smiled back at him, "I would really like that."

"Okay then, I'll be here to pick you up at four. Will that work for you?"

"I'll be ready and waiting," I said. We both smiled at each other. I closed the door and he put the car into gear. The window was down on his side of the car as I walked around the front. "Have a good night," he said.

"I already have, thank you," I said, with a slight smile on my face. He drove away and I was on cloud nine.

Later that evening, my sister arrived home. She walks in and I'm watching TV on the couch.

"I see you made it home okay," she said, closing the door behind her and locking it for the evening.

"Yes, I did and I made a new friend. He lives just around the corner from here and we hit it off so well, he wants to give me a ride to work tomorrow so we can continue our conversation," I told her.

"So what's his name?" she asked.

"Jason Robbe."

"Well, don't get your hopes up. Remember what you just went through back home with Bruce," she said, with a snide look on her face.

After a few days went by, I started to hear rumors at work. People were saying that it would never work between the two of us because we were so different. I was too nice and he was too much of a partier. They were all convinced, when I found out what that meant, that I'd definitely leave him. So whenever I would talk with people about how things were going between us, their response was always, "That's nice." Jason was also aware of the rumors that had started to wander around the office. He asked me out that Friday. I accepted.

He picked me up at home at around ten. Then we headed over to Golf-N-Stuff at the Metro-Center Mall. Before going inside, he said he wanted to talk to me. He turned the car off. It was an awkward moment of silence, before he spoke.

"I know you've been hearing rumors around the office, about me," he said, with his eyes glued to the steering wheel.

"Well, I've been hearing that our relationship wouldn't last very long due to your past," I said.

"That's what I want to talk to you about." He turned to look right at me with a very serious look on his face.

"Oooookay," I said slowly, not being sure I really wanted to hear what was going to come out of his mouth next. I was starting to get a little nervous and had goose bumps.

"I wanted it to be me that told you about my history. I didn't want you to find out from someone at work, namely, Lynette, who could blow it up into something more than it was," he said.

Now, I was curious more than anything. "Go ahead. Say what you need to say. I'm listening."

He grabbed the steering wheel and was very nervous. "Well, back in school, I met this guy, Joe. He became my best friend. We did everything together. We had the same friends and went to parties together." He started to get really nervous about what he was going to say next. "We started drinking and doing drugs together as well. I then found I could make good money by selling drugs. So I did. I was at a party one night that got busted by the cops. They found stuff on me and I went to jail."

I didn't know what to say at this point. All I could do was think about what everyone else had been saying. I started to wonder if I had gotten into a bad deal, again. I just kept quiet, looking straight ahead out the window and listened to the rest of what he had to say.

"While I was in jail, I saw a lot of things I never want to see again. I don't deal drugs anymore and I don't do drugs now either. It's hard sometimes when I go to parties with my friends. They try to get me to do things I don't really want to, but I don't want them not to like me anymore either," he said, very disappointed in himself.

"If they only like you because of drugs or alcohol, then they're not really your friends anyway," I said very sternly.

"Joe would never be that way with me. We've been through too much, but there are some others out there who would," he said. "Look, if you want me to just take you home now, I can do that. I just wanted you to hear it from me first."

There was silence that seemed to last forever. I turned to look at him. I had a very empty feeling inside and really didn't want to believe what I just heard. "Do you want to do drugs?" I asked, turning to look at him for his answer.

"No, I said I don't do that anymore. I've turned over a new page in my life. While I was in jail, I did have one good thing happen to me; I found God. I learned things that I never knew before. I was raised Catholic, but never really understood what they were saying or some of the things they did. I started to read the Bible and things started to click," he said. He had a very excited and scared look on his face. "Well, say something. I want to know what this does to our relationship. I like you a lot. You're different than the other girls I've dated in the past, and I like that," he said, with anxious curiosity.

At this point, I really didn't know what to say. I was very impressed with him finding God. At the same time though, could I trust him? Is he really telling me that he wants to change? The only way to find out was to take it slow and not to expect too much.

"Well, this isn't exactly what I was expecting to hear," I said. There was a long pause as he thought I was going to end it right then. I had to really think about what I wanted to do. "I guess the first thing I have to say is, I'm glad you found God. You do realize that drugs and alcohol will kill you eventually, right?" I asked.

He just nodded and shrugged his shoulders. I could see tears starting to swell up in his eyes, as he looked out the window on his side of the car.

"I'm very glad that you're the one who told me and I didn't find out from someone else. I don't drink or do drugs. I find other things to keep me happy." There was another long pause. "I understand that people make mistakes. I hope you've learned from yours. I will just say this, if I ever catch you going back on what you just told me, about not wanting to drink or do drugs anymore, then we'll be done," I said to him, without making too much of it. "Tell you what, we can be friends for now. Let's get to know each other better and see what happens from there. I don't mind having fun, but I also just got out of a very frustrating relationship."

"Agreed," he said. We started to get out of the car. "You're different than all the other girls I've ever dated. They either just want to party, spend my money, or get in bed." He paused for a minute thinking about what he had just said, as I stopped and looked over at him as well. "Not that that's what I do with everyone else; that's just what some girls want from me. Kinda makes me feel used."

"Well, I would think it should," I said. "I don't hang out with those kinds of guys."

"Glad to hear that!" he said. "Friends, then?"

"Friends," I said. "Now let's go have some fun!" We grabbed hands and started to walk toward Golf-N-Stuff. "So, does this place just have miniature golf?" I asked.

"What? You've never been to a Golf-N-Stuff before? Oh, you're gonna love this!" he said, as he opened up the two big heavy wooden doors. There were video games and pool tables galore, with food vendors and water bumper cars. Three full floors of nothing but every kind of game you could think of.

"Wow! We don't have anything like this back home," I said with a huge smile on my face. We had a great evening together. We played golf and of course he beat me.

When we went back to work on Monday, everyone learned that I had spoken to Jason about his past. Once they found out that I knew his past and things were still moving forward, they all backed off and wished us well, except my sister. She didn't think I should be dating him. I had been either getting rides from Dawn or riding the bus to get back and forth from school during the day, but I continued to ride with Jason to and from work, after that.

Jason looked a lot like Tom Cruise. He had the same stature, combed his hair the same as Tom Cruise did at that time, and was about the same height. When we would walk around in Metro-Center, I would hear girls yelling, "Tom, Tom, Tom." As they got closer and realized he wasn't Tom, they would just walk past and have a disappointed look on their faces. It happened a few times when I was with him. He loved it and I got such a kick out of it.

Most of the time, we'd go to Jason's house first after work, so he could change his clothes, before heading back out. It just so happened, that he still lived at home with his parents while trying to get back on his feet. He initially would ask me to wait in the living room and have me watch TV until he was ready. He'd spend half an hour in his room. I finally got up enough nerve to ask what he was doing, that took so long.

I walked over to his bedroom door and saw that it was just barely open. I peeked through first and saw him sitting in a chair just reading something. I knocked and he jumped and turned and looked to see me standing there.

"You've asked me every night to just wait here in the living room while you disappear into your bedroom for thirty minutes. I'm just a little curious; what are you doing in here?" I asked.

"I didn't know at first if I should tell you. I wasn't sure how you'd respond to what I was doing, but I think you'll understand now," he said. He invited me into his room. He had a Bible and notebook sitting on his bed with a devotional book next to it.

"You've been doing devotions, and you were afraid to tell me?" I asked, curiously surprised.

"Like I said before, most of the girls I would date would have thought I was some kind of weirdo or something. I didn't want to take that chance with you, until I knew for sure you'd be okay with it. It's kind of my thing to do with God."

"You never have to hide God from me. I would be honored, if you would let me in on your nightly devotions," I said, hoping he would feel comfortable enough to let me participate.

"You know, the Bible says if two or more people are gathered in one spot together worshiping, the Father is with you in the room," I said, hoping it would make a difference. I had never dated anyone I could talk about God with openly. I thought this was very cool.

"It would be nice to have someone to discuss things with during the devotion. Yes, we can start doing it tomorrow," he said with a smile, and then he took me home.

On the drive home, Jason said, "I wanted you to know that I'm going to be on TV soon." He looked over at me, while shifting gears.

"TV?" I said, with some confusion and interest. "What's that all about?" I asked.

"Well, awhile back I was up late and was watching TV. There was a guy who came on and had a show called *Sam Meranto's Mind Power.*

Anyway, he's an all-faith believer and does guided meditations to help you beat all kinds of bad habits, addictions, and plenty of things you want to change and make better in your life. I thought it couldn't hurt to try it, so I went to his place in Scottsdale and spoke to him. I told him what I had going on and that I needed help with getting the drug habit behind me. He's been helping me ever since. He made me some tapes that I listen to each night before bed. There are some to help me sell better at the job, have more self-confidence as well as the ones to help stay off drugs and stand up to temptations."

I just sat and listened to what he had to say. It was a short drive home, but it seemed to take a much longer time.

"I'd been going to his place before work on days you weren't with me. Sam asked if I wanted to do an interview on TV about my situation," he said with a smile. "I would like it if you would come with me and watch the taping. I'll introduce you to Sam as well. What do you think?" He listened, waiting intently to see what I'd say.

"I'd be happy to come with you and watch a TV show be filmed behind–the–scenes. I've never done that before, and it's right up my alley. I've told you how much I want to write movie scripts." I said with a very happy and curious tone. "When does this happen?" I asked.

"I'll have to let you know the actual filming date as it gets closer. We haven't got it set in stone just yet."

"Sounds like a plan," he said as he pulled up to my place.

Some nights I would invite him up to the apartment and we would talk for hours. Dawn didn't like this because we had classes the next day. She was always in her room.

I think it was about a week after that, when we actually went to Sam Meranto's place and did the filming. Everyone was so nice. I had a real blast there and while Jason was filming his TV spot, they asked if I wanted to try a session out myself. I didn't know what to say. I didn't have any real issues to get help with. They set me up with a very neutral session of confidence boosting to help me sell more at work. I wasn't sure how, or even if, it would help me at work, but it couldn't hurt while I was waiting. Sam had helped so many people with problems they were having. One big thing I thought was really cool was that he helped different stars over the years. He had pictures with so many people hanging up in his office. Sam has done a lot of good for a lot of very well known people that I had looked up to. I figured this had to be a good thing for Jason.

During the second trimester at school, it was about the second week into classes and I couldn't grasp anything the teacher was talking about. I started to wonder if I should be taking this class. I also realized that, since I was paying for school, I could also quit taking classes that I didn't want. I went to the counselor and talked about changing my major. I started to think about computer programming. It was something I could also use for making movies if I ever got to that point. We had put in for the change, but it would never come. I decided to finish the week out and just be done with the current classes.

I was sitting at the kitchen table in my apartment, trying to decide what to do about my homework that I just couldn't understand. My sister said, with an attitude, "Maybe if you spent more time doing your homework and less time over at Jason's, things would make more sense to you."

"You're not my mom, Dawn! I can go over there as much as I want," I responded.

"Well, I'm just telling you right now, that I don't want Jason over here after work anymore. I have homework to do and the two of you are too loud for me to concentrate. He's not welcome," she argued loudly.

"Hey, I pay rent here too, you know. I should be able to have my friends over if I want to. Who do you think you are, to say who I can or can't have over and when?" I said back to her, very upset.

She was in the kitchen with a towel in her hand and snapped it at me. The second time she did it, I grabbed the towel and pulled it out of her hands. She came at me and I backed up into the living room, waiting to see what she was going to do next. When she came at me, we got into a fight. We were supposed to go to work in half an hour and I was without a ride, at that point. Fortunately, I got a ride from our neighbors across the way, Keith and Randy. Dawn got to work before me. Everyone wanted to know what happened and why she had a black eye. She wouldn't tell them anything; I think because she knew she was in the wrong, so everyone asked me and I told them. I decided, at that point, I needed a new roommate.

I found some other students at school who needed help with their rent and moved in with them. They lived in the same complex, just on the north side instead of the south side. Eileen was her name. She became my best friend. I acquired two other roommates as well. One was Alan and the other was Tom. I lived with them for a while. Eileen and I eventually got our own place. We decided that Alan and Tom were a little too hard to clean up after. We moved into a new place not too far from where we were. We moved one street further north, to Bell Street. We were just across from the horse racetrack.

During all this time, Jason and I had started spending most of our time together. I started spending a lot more time over at his parents' house. He had two sisters. Chris is his older sister and Renee is his younger sister. Renee was still in high school. I got to know his mom and dad, Martha and Ed, who were very nice. We had gotten to know each other very well and shared a lot of the same interests. We were getting closer all the time, which I hoped would be a more permanent thing.

Chris would have lots of parties at her place. They usually involved alcohol and other things. These parties were ones that I would attend with Jason, but wasn't allowed into certain rooms. I was told it was "for my own protection." I always had my doubts about what that meant. There were times when I would be just sitting alone, for long periods. I always wanted to give him the benefit of the doubt, but I knew he wasn't a saint. As in every relationship, we had our ups and downs. We had more ups than downs, so I stayed with him.

We took rafting trips together, going down the Salt River with the MCI gang. That was fun. I went to Prescott a couple of times and we took a trip to California with a coworker, Hans. That was a fun trip! We went to Disneyland, Magic Mountain, and Universal Studios. That's one trip, I'll never forget! I went on my first roller coaster and one that even had a full loop in it. Hans and Jason got to be in a Star Trek type skit/play that was recorded and they both got copies to take home. We saw the Disney electric light parade at the end of the day and it was spectacular. We got so much closer, with each thing we did together.

Me and Jason with stuffed animals

During that summer, Jason had come up with an idea for a locking mechanism that could be used for off-road vehicles or motorcycles. Basically, anything that had a gas cap that could be accessed by someone and be tampered with. We spent a good portion of the summer, either at the college library, public library, or filling out copyright paperwork trying to make this happen. We got pretty far and had submitted the documents to the company that was going to help us get this manufactured. Jason was really hoping that we had a major breakthrough in the industry. It could make a lot of money. The research that we did showed no one else having this idea or technology on record. We were very hopeful.

We were spending so much time together we started to talk about moving our relationship to the next level. He wanted to get an apartment with me. I said that if we did that, I really wanted more of a lifetime commitment. He wasn't sure if he was ready for that. It made me wonder, if I was again in a dead-end relationship, that things would never go any further than where they were.

It also got me to thinking, about the parties that he'd taken me to over the last few months to meet his friends. All the times he disappeared and I was left alone to entertain myself with strangers. Why was I never taken with him into these "meetings" that he was having? Do I really know whom I'm with? Does he really care about me, the way he says he does? Questions like these just started wandering through my head.

October rolled around and we both went to work as Ninjas for Halloween. It worked so well together for us, having our outfits. What one of us didn't have, the other did. Both of us had been in martial arts classes growing up, so we accumulated a variety of items. Some accessories were not as accepted at work as others were. We had a lot of fun. We also found out that the movie *Days of Thunder* with Tom Cruise was going to be filming at the racetrack in Phoenix. We were both so excited! We wanted to go and see if we could pass Jason off as Tom Cruise.

We got bad news the night before they were to start filming. Jason's friend had been killed on Halloween and was having a funeral on that same day. He opted for the funeral instead. It was a very sad day. I found out much later that a couple of our coworkers were in the movie with Tom Cruise. They were working in the ambulance crew as EMTs on the racetrack, in case something went wrong. They said they would have gotten us in.

MCI had been talking about the telemarketing department going full time in November. This was great! Now, instead of just part-time hours it meant we'd finally have benefits as well as more money, for an apartment of our own. Jason and I had been competing for months for first place in sales. We always had competitions going on throughout the sales department and awards were given nightly as well as weekly and monthly. I had moved into the verifications department; it was an easier job, most of the time. Everyone was looking forward to Thanksgiving.

Just a week before Thanksgiving, we had gotten the paperwork for all of our new full-time benefits. Jason and I were filling them out together. We got to the part where it talked about life benefits.

"Well, we can afford a lot more, now that we're making more money. With the plans that we've been talking about, how do you want to work this?" I asked.

Jason and I studied the different policies we could sign for and decided on what should happen.

"We're not married yet. We should put someone down as beneficiaries who could really use the money, if something did happen to either of us. We get one time to change the policy through the year. If we do get married, we can change it," Jason said.

"I agree. It's a good plan. I think we should put our youngest sisters down as the beneficiaries. We can place ourselves as secondary and change it later. That way, they won't need to worry as much, if something happens to us. We're both very close to our younger sisters," I said. That's how the policies were filed. Neither of us thought this was ever going to be an issue.

CHAPTER 3

Thanksgiving

I t was Thanksgiving and MCI gave all the employees a four-day weekend. We were all so excited to be off work. Jason and I had decided to go see a movie after work on Wednesday night. We went to see *The Little Mermaid*. We both loved the movie. It's the fairy tale story that both of us were always looking for. We both wanted to find that one person we knew we could spend the rest of our lives with. We sat in his car after the movie and talked for probably an hour. Jason was my prince and I was his Ariel.

As we went home that night, we talked about the trip to Prescott, Arizona, where we were going to be spending Thanksgiving with his family. Jason's mom worked at a YMCA camp as a cook and got the family a cabin to stay in overnight.

About four weeks earlier, we had gone to a party where I met up with a couple of friends from Wasilla. We had so much fun, trying to catch up on our time since school, that we decided to throw a party for all the friends we could find. Friends who had gone to school in cities like Tempe, Phoenix, Flagstaff, or anywhere else that seemed close. Some were even in California who wanted to come. We had set up this party for the long weekend that everyone got for Thanksgiving. It was going to take place on Saturday, November 25. I was so excited! I was finally going to get to introduce Jason to some of the friends I grew up with.

Since we had gone full time at work, I also had been making plans to go back home for Christmas and was trying to get Jason to come with me, but he said he couldn't afford it. I couldn't understand how he couldn't afford the ticket now that he had more money. I knew my family would love to meet him. I would continue to ask him to join me in Alaska for Christmas.

We drove to Prescott on Thursday, November 23. We had a very nice drive up to the camp. When we got there, we got settled in with the cabin and met up with his mom. We consisted of Chris and her fiancé, Raymond; Renee; Jason's dad, Ed; and us. Jason had set up a horse trail ride for us to go out on. I hadn't been on a horse for a while, but I thought it should be a fun ride. Jason spoke to the female camp director most of the time on that trip. They hadn't seen each other in a while. I found myself also being a little on the jealous side, because the last two hours consisted of Jason talking almost entirely to her. I was left to take up the caboose, trying to keep up. I was a little sore after that ride. Needless to say, I was a little miffed when we pulled back up to the corral.

We put the horses up and thanked her for her hospitality. That's when Jason noticed I was a little too quiet.

"What's wrong? Didn't you have a good time?" he asked.

I replied, "Not exactly. I would like to have been included in your conversation, just a little more than I was. The only thing I really got from you was, "Are you okay back there?" when all I could see was the tail end of your horse. What am I supposed to think?"

"Don't get all jealous on me. We haven't seen each other in over a year and we were just catching up," he said.

"Let me guess; she was also one of the girls you used to date way back when," I replied, with a strong sarcastic tone.

"You wouldn't have been able to keep up with our conversation anyway. You weren't even around at the time to know what we were talking about. How are you supposed to stay in a conversation that you can't even contribute to?" he responded, sounding slightly frustrated and confused. "And yes, we did date a few times when I would come up to see mom."

At that point, I just shut up, shrugged my shoulders and started to walk to the main house. In the main house, you could smell all the cooking that had been going on the last couple of days. I took a deep breath and instantly got hungry. I could smell the hot roasted turkey, with all of its dressings and the yams with marshmallow toppings. There were rolls being baked and salads of all sorts. They had appetizers just sitting out for everyone to be able to munch on, while waiting for the main meal. I walked over and grabbed a couple of pickles and carrots. Meanwhile, Jason went in to the kitchen where his mom was heartily working.

"Hi Mom. How much longer until the food is ready for everyone?" he asked, as he tried to reach over and grab a roll off the pan.

Martha smacked Jason on the back of the hand, "Oh, no you don't! You can wait, just like everyone else. Dinner will be ready, in just a few minutes. If you can't wait, go grab something off one of the trays in the other room."

"Aw Mom, I just figured...." Jason started to say and was stopped in mid-sentence.

"You figured too much I think! You can just march yourself right out that door and sit at a table or go hungry," she said, with a slight smile on her face.

Jason was turning to head back out of the kitchen, when he leaned over and said, "Alright. I love you, Mom. Thank you so much for all the hard work that you put in. We all are going to appreciate it," he said very lovingly and gave her a kiss on the cheek.

Martha turned and looked at Jason with tears in her eyes, "Thank you dear. I would give you a hug, but I'm cooking right now. Now get out so I can go back to work and everyone can finally eat." She smiles at Jason, as he leaves the kitchen and walks back out to the dining hall.

"It won't be long now, before we can chow down on the turkey," he relayed to everyone who was in the dining hall. The line had started to grow quite long, by this time. About ten minutes later, the food was ready and there was a very nice prayer done by the pastor of the camp. We ate as much as we possibly could and then waddled our way back to the cabin, for some much-needed rest.

We relaxed at the cabin for a while, just resting for the evening ahead. As the night came on, we started to head back into town, along with everyone else. There was a Thanksgiving parade right down the middle of the highway. It looked a lot like a party town. There were people everywhere, drinking and smoking. I walked hand in hand with Jason. Both his sisters, Chris and Renee, were with us, as well as Raymond. Renee and I were the only ones not able to drink. There had been a few times where we were left outside bars, while the legal drinkers went inside for a bit. After a while, this started to get upsetting.

"Renee, are you ready to go back to the cabin?" I asked.

"Anything is better than just getting left in the middle of the street, with the other drunks," she replied.

As the group was coming out of the bar, I approached Jason. "I think Renee and I are ready to go back to the cabin."

"Why? What's the problem?" he asked, looking like there should be no problem. "This is a party night. You should live it up a little." He replied, with a smile and a nudge of his arm, while holding a beer in the other hand.

"I can't live it up a little. Not like you guys. I'm not old enough to enter those establishments and neither is Renee. Now, we could try getting in, but we're more than likely going to be kicked out. All of us, meaning you too," I said, with sarcasm in my voice. "If you want to party all night long, then take me and Renee back to the cabin. It's getting cold and we can't warm up in any of the places that are still open." I turned away from Jason, frustrated and upset that he couldn't understand the situation.

With my arms crossed and my foot tapping on the ground, I waited to hear a response to my next move. I could see my breath at this point, every time I exhaled. This is Arizona; it's not supposed to be this cold, I was thinking. I didn't bring gloves and a hat like I would in Alaska. I had to start rubbing my hands together to get them warm.

I turned around to see Jason, Chris, and Ray talking with a couple of other people. By this point, I was done with the situation and wanted the keys to the car, so I could at least go sit and listen to music, while I got warm.

I walked up to them. "Jason, can I just at least have the keys to the car? I really want to get warm. I'll listen to music and warm up, then you can just meet me there when you're done partying," I blurted out, as I was really starting to shake.

By this point, Jason could see how cold we were getting. He said, "No, let's all just go back to the cabin. We've had enough fun here. We've still got all weekend to have more fun, in a warmer place, too." He smiled and put his arm around me, trying to warm me up. "Happy Thanksgiving," he said with a smile and beer breath.

"Happy Thanksgiving," I replied. "I don't want to be a party pooper, but you've got to understand, it's cold out here!" I said, as we proceeded to walk back to the car.

We got back to the cabin and it was getting colder yet. The cabin was up on the mountain and you could feel the difference. When we got back to the cabin, everyone settled into the beds that were made for us. We watched a little TV, before finally going to sleep.

Upon waking up the next morning, we found that it had snowed overnight. Not much, just enough to cover the ground in white. Less than half an inch if I remember correctly. We all took turns in the bathroom. Then packed the car up with all our personals. We went over to the main hall, one more time, for breakfast. Martha was staying for one more day, to help with the cleanup. Jason and I had plans coming up, and I needed to get back to call and confirm the people who would be coming to our party.

Ed and Renee came in a separate car as well as Chris and Raymond. Everyone left before we did.

We thanked everyone who allowed us to stay with them. We then began our trip back to Phoenix. As we got back on the road, to head down the mountain, the car started to slide a little. "Oh crap! This isn't going to be good!" Jason loudly stated, a little panic-stricken.

"What?" I asked loudly, startled by his reaction. I grabbed the bar on the side of the door to steady myself. "Is this going to be a problem for you to drive in?" Not being sure, if I needed to be a little alarmed or not.

"No. It's just that with this car having all-wheel steering, it makes it a little tricky to keep control, compared to a car that doesn't have it. We'll be fine once we get to the bottom of the hill. I'll just take it very slow," he stated in a calm, collected voice, as to not to alarm me. By

Jason sitting on rock wall

the time we reached the city portion of Prescott, the snow was melting and the road was wet. We were both very relieved to see this.

We had a very nice return trip home. The weather was clear and warm. The view was astounding. The music and company was satisfying. We even got to watch a very large tarantula cross the road in front of us. This weekend had started out really well and I was so happy. I couldn't wait for Saturday to get here.

The journey took about two to three hours. We arrived home early Friday afternoon and started to put our things away.

CHAPTER 4

Preparations

E very Saturday we washed and detailed Jason's car, but this time, we wanted to do it a day ahead just to be ready. Today, we even waxed the car. You know how first impressions are. He wanted to make a very good one with my friends. We worked on it for about two hours after arriving home.

During this time, Jason's best friend, Joe Massamillo, came over. He was pulling a trailer to show Jason his three-wheeler. I continued to clean the car. He went over to talk with Joe, for a bit. I needed to make a call to my sister about the party, so I told Jason I'd be back in a few minutes.

I went inside the house and made the call to my sister.

"Hello," she said.

"Hi Dawn, it's Chery. I was wondering how many people you were able to get a hold of for the party tomorrow."

"Quite a few actually. Some may come, but I couldn't get a confirmation from everyone," she said.

"Do we know how many people will be there?"

"No. There are too many other people calling as well. We won't know for sure, until we get there. Which reminds me, can I get a ride from you guys? I don't know how to get to the party and I think Jason said he knew exactly where it was."

"I don't think it's a problem. I'll ask for sure and let you know, but I'm sure it'll be fine," I said.

"Cool," she said, pleased and relieved.

"Okay, I'm going to head back outside and finish cleaning the car. Joe came over while we were cleaning the car and they have been outside talking ever since. I better find out what's up. He had a three-wheeler with him," I said, with a curious tone. "I'll call you again later."

"Okay, talk to you then," she said.

"Bye," I said, and hung up the phone.

I went back outside. They were just finishing their conversation. Jason was walking toward me as Joe was pulling away in his truck.

"What did Joe want?" I asked curiously.

"Did I ever tell you that Joe and I use to race three-wheelers in competitions?" he said. He walked over to where his three-wheeler was parked, in front of the car and covered with a tarp and bungee cords.

"No. I don't think you have. We have one back home that I use to run around on, but just for fun. Nothing else," I said.

"Well, Joe and I had the top gear and everything. I still have it somewhere. I think it's in the shed," he said, trying to remember where he stored it. "The reason Joe stopped by is, he wants to take the machines out tomorrow for a little ride. We haven't done that in years," he said, excitedly.

"Wait just a minute now," I said. I was a little miffed at this interruption to our plans. "We already have plans for tomorrow. The party...remember?" I said, frustrated.

"I know. I told Joe that you've been putting this party together for about a month now. He said that we could go out in the afternoon and have plenty of time to get back to get ready for the party," Jason said in a very matter-of-fact tone. "I really want to do it. We haven't been out on these for a long time. I think it would be fun," he said. I didn't think it was a good idea. I just had this bad feeling that something wasn't right about it and it would affect me getting to the party on time. I'm supposed to be one of the hosts and I can't be late.

"I don't have a good feeling about this Jason," I said, being frustrated and disappointed that he could take on something with his friends so quickly, when he knew how much this meant to me. "What time does he want to leave?" I asked.

"I think we'd be heading out about one o'clock. It takes about forty-five minutes to get where we are going, in a wash area. It gives us about two hours of riding before heading back for the party," he said reasonably. Then he got a little on the quiet side. "Why is it, when my friends want to go do something, you always have this 'bad feeling' that something is going to go wrong? It's almost like you don't want to be around them at all," he said.

"That's not it at all," I said back to him, firmly. "Yes, it's true that I don't approve of all that your friends do, and try to get you to do with them, but I do like them very much, especially Joe. Is Christy coming with us then too?" I asked. Christy was Joe's wife. She was also someone Jason used to date before me. Jason and I went to their wedding in Tucson earlier in the year. Christy got pregnant, so she and Joe got married.

"Yes, she'll also be riding with Joe," he said.

There was a long silence as Jason waited for me to come to a decision on what to do about this. We finished the car. When that was done, Jason walked up to me and asked in a soft voice, "Well, what do you think? If I promise that I will get you back here to your party, on time, will you go?" He grabbed both of my hands and just held them, while waiting for the answer. Again, I sat there, pondering what I should do. And, as I always do with the ones I care about, I gave in.

"Yes, I'll go with you," I said.

"Yes, yes," he said with a big smile.

"Now, don't get too happy just yet. You have to make sure that I make it to this party. If I don't make it to this party on time, there will be serious consequences," I said sternly. "Now, while you were talking with Joe, I talked to Dawn. She wants a ride to the party. I told her I didn't think that it'd be a problem. Are you okay with that?"

Smiling, more like beaming, he said, "Yes, that's fine. We'll pick her up too." He gave me a very big hug and said, "Now, there's so much to do. I haven't had this thing going in years. I need to find the helmets, buy new spark plugs, and..." He had started to ramble. I stopped him in mid-sentence.

"Jason, I know you have a lot to do to get ready for this, but so do I. You go to the store and buy what you need and I'm going to jump on the phone and call as many people as I can." I was trying to calm him down.

We split ways for a few hours getting things ready for both of our events. I still didn't have a warm fuzzy feeling about this. Jason took me back to my apartment where I lived with Eileen. She was just getting settled into our new place downtown that was closer to work. After making a few phone calls, I needed to get clothes for riding. As I looked around my room, everything seemed to be dirty.

"How can almost everything I own be dirty?"

"Well, maybe if you came home once in a while and did laundry, you would have something clean to wear," said Eileen. She then smiled at me and said, "Why don't you take a pair of my jeans and get them back to me when you're done?" She picked out a pair that she knew would fit and threw them at me.

"These are your favorite jeans. Are you sure that you want me to wear these out on a three-wheeler?" I looked up at her.

"Sure, they're just pants. If you do, by some weird chance ruin them, you can go buy me that new pair I've been looking at," she said with a smile. The new pants she was talking about were very expensive, but looked great on her.

"Okay, thanks. I'll make sure that I take very good care of your favorite jeans." I packed up what I needed into a bag. Jason was only supposed to be gone for a little bit. He went to the store to get the parts he needed for the three-wheeler. I sat down on my bed and looked at Eileen. I asked, "Are you going to be able to make it to the party tomorrow?"

"I don't think so. I've got other plans already and I have to follow through on those. Although, I would love to meet your friends from Alaska," she replied.

"Well, I don't think there's a time limit on this party. If you get finished with your plans and still want something to do, come on over and check out what's happening." Just then, there was a knock at the front door.

"I'll get it. It's probably Jason coming back for me." I picked up my bag and gave Eileen a hug, as I went to the front door. She followed me out into the main room of the apartment. I looked through the peephole and sure enough, it was Jason. I opened the door.

"Did you get all your parts?" I asked, with a hopeful look.

As he stepped into the apartment, he said, "Hi Eileen. How's it going?" Then he looked at me and said, "Yes, I found everything to get it running for the day."

"I'm fine," Eileen replied. "You make sure to bring her back intact, okay? She's wearing my favorite jeans." She was smiling the whole time.

He looked over at me puzzled and with a smile said, "What is that supposed to mean?"

"I didn't have any clean clothes, so Eileen let me borrow one of her pairs of jeans. She said if I was here more, I wouldn't have to worry about that so much." We both just smiled and looked over at her.

"I guess that might be true," he said. He turned to me, "We'll have to work on that somehow. Are you ready to go? Did you get all that you need for tomorrow?"

"I have all the items I need for our trip and I think all the clothes for the party are already at your place," I responded.

Jason said, "I guess we're off then." I waved to Eileen, as I shut the door and thanked her again one more time, for the use of the jeans. We walked down to the car and put the bag in the backseat and drove back to his parents' house.

When we got there, we still had a lot of work to do on the three-wheeler. I put my clothes away in the house and went back out to help.

"What can I do to help?"

Jason had already taken the tarp off the machine and laid it down, inside the carport. "Not much for right now, but I'll let you know when I do," he said.

"How about some music while you're working?"

"Sure, that would be great! Did you want to just turn the car on and open the sunroof or get a radio?"

"I think the car should be fine. We're right here anyway," I said. He gave me the keys and I turned it on and opened the sunroof. I love good music, doing anything. It helps me get things done faster, for whatever reason. Not too long after, Jason asked me to get something that he thought was under the tarp.

"If you lift up that tarp be careful; it may have a black widow under it. They like to hide under things like that," he said.

"Great." I just kicked it up a little and said, "No, it's not here." He found what he needed and continued. Jason changed the oil, spark plugs, and tried to tighten the gears. We got more gas and had some even left over. The three-wheeler was ready. Now, we needed to find the gear he used to wear.

"If I remember correctly, I think that I put it all in the shed here outside my window." He opened the gate to the area outside his window that had a small shed and storage area for bikes and things. It didn't look to me like it had been opened for a while. We managed our way through all the junk and opened the lock on the front of the shed. It was full of all kinds of things.

"I'm not going in there," I said, being afraid of more spiders. "Who knows what's in there?" I was thinking.

"I don't want you to anyway. You don't even know what you're looking for."

"Here, hold this." He handed me the lock. "What I do want you to do is, grab the things that I'm going to hand to you." He stepped inside the shed.

I shrugged my shoulders and said, "Okay."

He began to look through boxes and bags and found two helmets that he had used. One was much newer than the other. He had found gloves, shin guards, elbow guards, and clothing that they used to wear while racing.

"Are you really going to wear all this? We're just riding out in the area for fun, not for racing," I said, hoping I was right about that. I'm going to be riding with him after all.

"No, I'm not wearing all of this," he said sarcastically. "Just some of it. I just found all of it together, so I grabbed everything." He stared at the items to see if they were even usable. "I'm not sure if this old helmet will even fit me anymore. Maybe we can clean it up and you can see if it will fit you." He rotated it over and over in his hands, to see if there were any cracks.

"I'm not putting that thing on my head until it's cleaned up," I said with my hands on both hips. It was covered in spider webs and dirt, from lying on the floor of the shed.

Jason then went ahead and cleaned up all the items he decided to take for our protection. I tried on the older helmet and it was tight, but it worked. The other helmet was a top-of-the-line helmet, for that time. It fit him like a glove. We packed the items into the Prelude trunk and were ready for the trip the next day.

CHAPTER 5

The BIG Day!

I think we woke up around ten on Saturday. It was sunny and pleasantly warm. We got up and made a full healthy breakfast. It started with scrambled eggs and sausage and bacon. Toast was perfectly browned and buttered. Glasses of orange juice were poured and placed on the table. Anyone who was hungry in the house, at that point, was welcome to have some if they wanted. We were listening to the radio while making breakfast, dancing and singing the whole time and loving every minute of it.

On the other end of the kitchen, was a small room that had been turned into a workout place for Jason. It had a bench press, stationary bike, and free weights. We had talked about starting a workout routine, so that I could get to the weight I wanted to be at and look more trim. We just hadn't started it yet. At that time, I was 5 feet 9 inches tall and weighed about 140 pounds. I was 125 pounds when I graduated, which wasn't that long ago.

I was still a little nervous about trying to cram too much into one day, but I was very excited at the same time.

We got ourselves ready for Joe to meet up with us. He was bringing his trailer over that would fit both three-wheelers. He also owned a truck to pull the trailer to where we needed to go.

We were sitting in the living room watching a little TV when the doorbell rang.

Jason got up and walked over to open the door. "Hey Joe," he said.

"Morning Jason. Are you and Chery ready to head out?" Joe asked, very excitedly and rubbing his hands together.

"Yeah, come on in." He opens the door some more to let Joe in, while Christy decided to stay in the vehicle waiting for us. "Chery and I have everything in the trunk and we just need to load up my three-wheeler and we should be good to go." Jason closes the door behind Joe.

I got up from the couch, "Hi Joe, where's Christy?" I asked.

"Oh, she's just waiting in the truck," he said. Joe could smell the food we had just been making.

"What smells so good? You guys made breakfast, didn't you?" Joe cleaned up the last of what was sitting on the table and looked satisfied.

We cleaned up our dishes from breakfast and turned off the TV. I grabbed my purse from the bedroom, made one last bathroom stop, and we headed out the door.

"Mom, Dad, we're heading out now. We'll be back later. Love you!" Jason yelled, loud enough for his parents to be able to hear us.

"Be careful," his mom yelled from her room at the back of the house.

As I walked outside, I could see Christy sitting in the truck and waved at her. She was listening to music and waved back at me. I couldn't tell what she was listening to, but it had a lot of base in it. I watched as Jason and Joe got the three-wheeler started and put it up onto the back of the trailer. It only took about five minutes to get this done and we were heading out.

Jason got in the car, just as I was getting in as well. "It's about forty-five minutes to where we're heading, so we'll stop at the Circle K store and get something to drink and eat on the way," he said.

"Okay, that sounds like a good plan. Where are we going anyway?" I asked, curiously.

"We're heading out to a wash area called Cave Creek Wash at Needle Point. It's just for off-road vehicles. Joe and I have been there lots of times. It has a lot of trails for us to try out." He sat back in his seat and just had this look of deep thought on his face. "Man, I haven't been out there in years," he said softly. He turned to look at me. "Being from Alaska, you should love this!" He smiled.

He started the car and turned up the radio to some great music. We loved listening to the radio and the eighties music. It's always great when you can listen to music that will take you back to that one particular day or time, when you can remember what you were doing when you heard it.

It was a long drive out to the wash area. Not much to see, but open land and sand. The road that we drove, getting us to the parking area, was very sandy, almost to the point of the car getting stuck. All I could think of was, "Please don't let us get stuck out here. This is out in the middle of nowhere and I'll miss the party tonight." Jason could obviously see the slight bit of panic on my face and said, "Don't worry. If we get stuck, Joe can pull us out with his truck. He brought a tow cable, just in case we needed it for something." He put his hand on my leg and said, "Just relax. Everything will be just fine."

We got to the spot that they wanted and parked both vehicles. When we arrived, there was a lake in front of us, with some people who were trying to drive their vehicles across it. One of them barely made it and the other one got stuck about three-quarters of the way across. The first truck pulled out a tow cable and was trying to pull the second truck out while they sat in the water and just spun their tires.

"What a stupid thing to try to do," I said. "Didn't they realize that the water was too deep for that truck to make it through?"

Jason, Joe, and Christy had also been watching the chaos from behind me. "Some people just don't know when to quit," Joe said, turning and walking away as we all started shaking our heads.

"Well, let's get this party started!" Jason said, rubbing his hands together as they untied the ropes for tie-downs. Jason and Joe got the two three-wheelers off the trailer and we took out all our gear from the trunk.

"Which trail should we try first?" Jason asked.

"Let's try the one that goes down next to the lake a ways and go from there," Joe replied. Christy got on with Joe, I got on the back with Jason, and away we went. We spent the next two hours riding every trail we could find. It was a lot of fun! We went back to the car about three-thirty and took a break to get food and drinks.

"When do you think we should head back?" I asked.

After taking a bite of a sandwich and a drink from his bottle, Jason replied, "Well, it took us about an hour to get here, so if we leave by four or so we should have plenty of time to get ready for the party tonight." He took another drink "I think there's still one more trail that we haven't gone down yet. Right, Joe?" he said, pointing to the one just up from where the cars were sitting.

"Yeah, we haven't gone down there yet and it isn't a very long trail. We should be back in half an hour, easy," Joe replied.

"I'm getting a little tired. I think I'm going to stay here at the car for this one," said Christy.

"Well, if we are going to do this, then let's get going," I replied. We walked over to the three-wheeler and I got on first. Jason had my helmet in his hands looking it over.

"How well does this thing really fit you?" he said, starting to look concerned.

"It's tight, but it does fit and it'll work for me," I replied. "Why do you ask?"

"I'd rather you wear my helmet on this last trip out. I'd feel better if you had on the good helmet."

"But then, what are you going to use? That smaller helmet doesn't fit you."

Jason replied, "Don't worry about me. I'll be fine. I just won't wear one on this last trip out."

"Why don't you wear the good helmet, since you're in front? If I see anything that looks like it's going to hit me, I'll just duck in behind you. After all, you're in front of me and will take the brunt of whatever it is that's in the way." Feeling confident in what I had just said.

"No! I don't want you to not wear a good helmet!" he said.

"Okay, I'll wear the one I've been wearing and you keep the good helmet!" I said.

"Quit arguing with me! If you don't put on the good helmet, then I'll put it on you myself!"

At that point, I knew he was serious. "Fine. I'll wear the good helmet," I said, and put it on. Jason walked over to the car and put the smaller helmet in the trunk. He walked back over and got on, sitting in front of me.

"Let's do this!" Jason said. He started up the machine and so did Joe. We headed down the last trail of the day. This trail had lots of trees and was full of sand. It made for good sliding around the corners. Lots of fun for the guys, and I just had to hold on for dear life. We hadn't gotten too far down the trail when Joe's machine started to sputter and eventually just quit on him. We had been riding behind Joe, following his lead and Jason passed Joe when his machine quit.

"Why don't you stop and help him get it started up again! Don't just leave him there!" I yelled, over the noise of the running three-wheeler.

Jason made a U-turn in the path and headed back to where Joe had stopped. Joe had already taken a couple of things apart and was trying to desperately figure out what happened. Jason got off our machine and went to help while I stayed put. I watched them play with spark plugs and other things. Then Jason had an idea. He took the dipstick and rubbed it in the sand, then put it back in. The three-wheeler started right back up. I thought for sure, it wasn't going to run now. I didn't understand what he had just done, but it worked, so I was happy with that. Jason ran back to our machine and hopped on. We took off, in front of Joe this time.

I LOVE JASON on rock wall

As we turned into the corner, there was a rock wall in front of us, and trees to the right of us. It was sandy with a 90degree corner, turning to the right. On the rock wall, someone had spray painted the words "I LOVE JASON." Between the "I" and "JASON," the word love was represented by the shape of a heart. It was all in white. When we both saw this, we turned and looked at each other.

I smiled at him as I pointed to the wall and yelled over the three-wheeler, "I LOVE YOU!" He smiled back and said "I LOVE YOU TOO!" I gave him a big squeeze as we went into the 90-degree corner. That's the last thing I ever got to say to Jason and the last thing I would remember.

CHAPTER 6

The Accident

P eople who were involved with the accident contributed the information in this chapter. These would be friends, family, Joe, and people who were at the scene, as well as at the hospital. I won't remember anything for about two to three weeks after, so this is the information I compiled.

I still don't remember hearing or seeing anything.

As we went into the 90-degree corner, a GMC step-side pickup truck was coming in the opposite direction. They had been traveling at a fairly high rate of speed, getting ready to use the soft sand to throw the tail end of their truck around the corner, as to not hit the rock wall.

The police report estimated the point of impact to be about fifty miles per hour. The truck was raised up higher than the legal limit. When you are sitting on a three-wheeler, the bumper then comes up to your face.

The truck hit us head-on. He had cut the corner as sharp as he could to swing the tail end of his truck around. Upon impact, Jason was killed instantly. The impact crushed his chest. He would have died no matter if he were wearing a helmet or not. He fell off to the right side and landed in the ditch. I was thrown back fifteen feet and landed head first, crushing my helmet in three places.

Joe was right behind us as this took place. He saw the whole thing happen. He had to dodge the truck, so as not to be hit by him as well.

"NOOOOOOOOOOOOO!" he yelled at the top of his lungs as he swung back around to see what had just happened.

He took his helmet off as fast as he could. He looked back at the truck, which had actually driven up over the top of the three-wheeler and had to be put into reverse, to get back off of it. There were a few people in the car. The passengers all jumped out of the truck and ran. As the driver tried to do the same, Joe said, "Oh no you don't! You son of a..." He jumped on the driver and tackled him. He was not going to let him get away.

"What the hell did you just do?" he yelled. Joe was so upset and out of control; he was hitting the guy and and angrily shaking him.

Not too far away, a group of people who were hiking heard the whole thing happen. They ran over to the scene as fast as they could get there. The group consisted of two EMTs and some people from the media. They were a Christian group of friends out enjoying the day. They were trying to take a break from their normally busy daily lives, until this happened.

Upon arriving, they started to evaluate the scene.

Looking at Joe first, "Are you okay?" Some of them ran over to me, and the EMTs to Jason.

Joe responded with anger, "Yeah I'm fine! I think Jason is dead, and Chery is making gurgling noises. I'm not getting off this guy though! He hit them with his truck!" Joe continued to hold the driver down. The driver was squirming to get away, but without much luck.

"Hey, a couple of you guys go over and help him keep this guy in custody until the police get here," yelled one of the men in the group. "Someone needs to go get help. It's a long ways away. I don't know if it will matter, but we have to try," yelled out one of the other rescuers in the group.

One of the media guys ran off to get help. I think he was going to head back into town. The two EMTs went over to Jason first to check him out. Most of the group was already leaning over him. When they all realized that he was already dead and there was no saving him, they turned their attention over to me. I was alive and still gurgling, with blood coming out of my mouth. Before leaving Jason's body, the entire group all looked up at each other. One of the men asked, "Does anyone else feel that?" Everyone just looked at each other in awe. Then realized they needed to be over with me.

"Chery. Chery, can you hear me?" Joe asked. "Don't worry, we're going to help you, as much as we can anyway."

All that was heard was more grunting from pain and the gurgling of blood in my throat. The EMTs did what they could to help me get comfortable and to work on the injuries I had. Nobody thought that I'd survive. We were just too far out, with no way of contacting anyone for help.

It was about that time that they heard a helicopter flying over. They were on their way to another site. They decided to take a different route to that location and ended up flying right over the top of the accident.

"Hey, look at that," said the copilot to the pilot. "Do you see that? It looks like it just happened."

"I'll check it out," said the pilot. He turned to head to where we were at, as he called into the base for a response on the scene. "HQ, this is HELO ONE, Do you copy?"

"HELO ONE, this is HQ. Go ahead," they responded.

"Yeah, we're on route to our present destination when we came across an accident that looks like it has just happened. It's at the wash area at Needle Point. Has this been reported yet?"

"Negative. There has been no report of an accident out there, at this time," she responded. "Does this look like it's serious?"

"Yes, very serious, and I'm going to land and check it out. It appears a 4x vehicle has hit a three-wheeler with two passengers. Both are lying on the ground and could possibly be deceased. Please send backup and an ambulance ASAP! It also appears the driver has been taken into custody by someone at the scene. Please send police now. HELO ONE out," said the pilot.

"10-4 HELO ONE, police and an ambulance are on their way. Good luck. Keep us posted on your status. We will get coverage for your original destination, from another location. HQ out."

The pilot looked for an open spot large enough to set the chopper down. When he landed, the co-pilot hopped out of the chopper first and ran over to the group. He began to take over the situation and asked, "What happened?"

Joe chimed in, trying to compose himself from crying so much. "They were just heading into the corner when this guy comes flying around the corner and cuts into it. Hitting them head-on! I saw the whole thing!" He started to cry uncontrollably. One of the women from the group tried to console him as best she could. "Someone needs to go tell Christy what happened. She's at the car waiting for us to come back," Joe said, as he fell to the ground, still unable to believe what just happened to us.

"Yes, I'll go get her. What does the car look like that she'll be standing next to?" she asked.

"It's the red Honda Prelude, right at the entrance to this trail. How do I tell her what happened? I was in front until my machine stopped.

They helped me start it and took off. It should have been me in the front, not them," said Joe.

The nice woman who had been helping Joe went to get Christy and told her what happened. She made sure there was someone else there to help with Joe first.

"The accident hadn't been reported when we flew over. There's help on the way. I don't think we can wait for them with Chery though. She looks pretty torn up," the co-pilot said, as he was checking me over.

The pilot came running up next to the scene with a bag in one hand. "What's the situation?"

"Well, the boyfriend is dead upon impact. The girlfriend is alive, but barely. She sustained very traumatic head injuries from being thrown fifteen feet and landing on her head. She has a broken jaw and has blood coming from her mouth with gurgling sounds. Not sure if there are any internal injuries at this time," he responded as calmly as he could.

"Has anyone tried to remove the helmet?" the pilot asked.

"No. We didn't want to move her too much. We didn't know how bad she would be with hitting her head first." Joe said.

"We really need to get this off. It's already shattered in three spots, so it shouldn't be too hard to remove. I need someone to hold her head very still." The pilot then slowly pulled the helmet off, with the co-pilot holding my head very steady.

"Okay, get the boyfriend covered. Let's get her stable enough to fly back to the hospital in Scottsdale." He started to get a stretcher ready for transport. During the process of getting me ready to fly, my heart stopped.

The pilot yelled, "She's flat-lining! Get the paddles! HURRY!" They pulled out the portable unit and quickly placed the pads on my chest and grabbed the paddles.

"CLEAR!" he yelled, as he sent electric shock through my body to try to revive my heart. Everyone pulled away from me, as the shockwave went through my entire body, lifting me up off the ground for only a split second. Nothing!

"Hit me again!" They pumped up the machine again. "CLEAR!" This time they got a heartbeat. "Okay, we've got her back. Let's get her in the chopper and head out," yelled the pilot. They got everything packed back up, loaded me into the chopper, and we were off to the hospital.

On the way to the hospital, I flat-lined again. They were able to revive me once more. They knew there wasn't much time left for me.

"I'm going to head to Scottsdale Memorial Hospital-Osborn. It's the closest one," yelled the pilot back to the co-pilot, who was with me in the back of the helicopter still keeping an eye on how I was doing.

"HQ, this is HELO ONE, come in." The pilot waited for a response.

"HELO ONE, this is HQ; go ahead. We've been waiting to hear back on your report," the dispatcher responded.

"We are bringing in one of the casualties from the scene. She's very combative and unable to communicate with us. She has flat-lined on us twice already. She has a severe head injury with a broken jaw. Her boyfriend was killed upon impact and is still out at the scene. We don't know if she has any internal bleeding, but she was bleeding from her mouth. Could be from the jaw being broken. We will need an immediate trauma room as soon as we arrive. HELO ONE out." The pilot turned to look back and see that I was still with them.

"We will be ready and standing by upon your arrival HELO ONE. HQ out." Then there was silence, except for the sound of the chopper blades cutting the air.

Meanwhile, back at the accident scene, when the police arrived they had found the driver still being held down by Joe and a few others. Upon investigation of the accident, the police found that the driver had been out earlier in the day and was off-road driving while drinking and ran into a tree branch. The branch went through the driver's side of the windshield and left a huge hole in it. Since the driver had been drinking, they took the Budweiser beer carton and opened it up completely. They duct-taped it to the inside portion of the driver's side window, extending across over half the windshield, so the windshield wouldn't fall in on him while he was driving. How this person was able to drive the truck after that is beyond me. You would have to have your head out the window or lean clear over to the passenger side of the vehicle to see where you were going. Amazing! Not only had this guy been drinking, and was drunk when they found him, but the police also found evidence of pot and pipes on the truck floorboard. You would think that with all this evidence, he'd be put away for a long time. I'll let you know later how that all turned out.

There were four people in the truck initially when he hit us. Three of them jumped out and ran. They just went back to the campsite where they had been with others all day. The police found them there, after they arrested the driver. I believe it was his wife and two kids. That's what I was told anyway. I also learned that the breath test was done wrong or something. They didn't have anything they could use to hold him on that. He had a history of drinking and driving though. Maybe it had been too long before the police got there or something; I don't really know. He was charged with manslaughter and aggravated assault. No mention of the drug use either or driving in an unauthorized area.

CHAPTER 7

Friends and Family

I n the meantime, my sister Dawn had been waiting for a phone call from me, to let her know when I would pick her up for the party. When she hadn't heard anything and time was getting short, she made a phone call to Jason's house and asked if we had returned from the ride.

"We haven't seen or heard from anyone since they left this morning," said Chris. "I'm starting to wonder what's happening as well. Jay (Jason) doesn't usually leave us hanging like this. Let me make a couple of calls and I'll call you back, Dawn."

"Okay, I'll call you if I hear anything either." Dawn hung up the phone, seeming a little nervous about the whole situation.

Just as Chris hung up her phone, a call rang through. Chris picked up the phone, thinking that it was probably the call they'd been waiting for. "Hello."

"Hello, this is the admitting desk for Scottsdale Memorial Hospital-Osborn; is this the residence of Jason Robbe?" Chris instantly got chills all over her body and went to sit down. "Yes, this is his sister, Chris. Is everything alright?" she asked, not really sure she wanted to hear what they were going to say.

"There has been an accident and I think you want to get to the hospital as soon as you can. There was a girl with him and you may want to contact her family as well."

"I'll contact her sister and we will be there soon. Thank you." Chris hung up the phone. She sat in the chair for what seemed like an eternity but was actually only a couple of seconds. She yelled through the house to her parents that there had been an accident and that Jason was involved. She then picked up the phone again and called Dawn back.

"Hello."

"Hi Dawn, this is Chris." By now Chris was in tears, thinking of all that could be wrong.

"Is everything alright?" Dawn asked, scared and curious as to why Chris was crying.

"No, I don't think so. I just got a call from Scottsdale Memorial Hospital saying that there's been an accident. They said both Jason and Chery have been involved in it and that we need to get to the hospital quickly." Chris sobbed a little more.

"Oh no! I don't know how to get there," Dawn stated in a panic.

"Don't worry, Ray and I will come pick you up on our way, in just a few minutes. You're ready, right?"

"Yes, I was ready for the party, so I'm good. I'll see you in a few minutes. Thanks." Dawn hung up the phone. She thought about calling my mom, but without knowing all the facts first, she didn't want to upset her and decided to wait.

Dawn said that Ray was driving so fast through traffic she thought they would get into an accident as well. She was very nervous about the ride and they were all trying to not read too much into the call Chris had gotten, but it was hard not to think bad thoughts, because of the way the nurse's voice was on the phone.

When they arrived at the hospital and announced who they were, Dawn, Ray, and Chris were all put into a waiting room to see a doctor. Martha, Ed, and Renee would all show up soon after. The doctor enters the room.

"Which of you is related to Jason Robbe?" the doctor asked, looking at everyone in the room.

Chris spoke first and said, "I'm his sister. Is he okay?"

"I'm afraid not." He paused. "Jason has died in a car accident with the three-wheeler he was riding on." Everyone in the room gasped and Chris covered her mouth and turned into Ray's chest; he held her and comforted her, while the rest of the information was given.

"Where's my sister, Chery?" Dawn demanded.

"Your sister is in the Intensive Care Unit (ICU) with extensive injuries to her face, head, and left leg. She has been very combative and has been hard to restrain right now. We are still working with her on getting her stabilized. My name is Dr. McFarland and I will be doing my best to keep you all informed on how she's doing," he said.

"Where is Jason?" Dawn asked.

"As far as I know, he's still at the scene of the accident. Chery was brought in by helicopter. She's very lucky the pilots decided to take a detoured route to their original destination. She would not have made it without them finding her first. They'll be bringing Jason in by ambulance later."

"I need to call my mom in Alaska. Where can I use a phone?" Dawn asked.

"Come with me and I'll get you one you can use," said Dr. McFarland.

Dawn instead called her roommate and then her roommate called my mom.

It was late Saturday afternoon when the call came in from the hospital that no mother ever wants to receive.

"Hello," said my mom, Janice.

"Hello, is this Dawn's mom?"

"Yes."

"Dawn wanted me to call you. I'm her roommate and there's been a terrible accident with her sister, Chery." She could hear the gasp come from my mom, before proceeding with the rest of the information. "I don't know a lot about what happened, but Jason is dead and Chery is missing teeth with other severe injuries and she's in the hospital."

"Was Dawn with them when this happened?" She knew that there was supposed to be a get-together of some of the friends from Wasilla, that night.

"No, it happened before the party was supposed to begin. Dawn is at the hospital right now though. That's why she had me call you instead. She's trying to keep up with all that's happening there."

"Thank you for the call. Tell her I'll be there as soon as I can." She hung up the phone. Immediately upon getting off the phone, she told her husband Rudy what had happened and fell to the floor in disbelief and tears. She managed to get herself together and start packing to catch the first flight to Phoenix.

My younger sister, Wendy, was working at Starvin Marvin's Pizza in Wasilla when my mom called to tell her what was going on. She asked for time off and went to Phoenix as well. They bought their very expensive, last minute tickets, at the airport counter. Mom asked if there was any help they could get with the emergency trip they had to take. The response was not what she was ready to hear.

"If you can bring us a death certificate only, then we can give you a discounted rate."

My mom wasn't sure what to say. She didn't even know if I'd be alive by the time they got to Phoenix. Wendy and Mom cried their way to

Phoenix and were picked up at the airport by my roommate, Eileen, and went straight to the hospital.

When they got to the hospital and entered the room I was in, my mom said I looked terrible. I had a neck brace on, breathing tubes in my mouth, and no movement as I was in a coma by now. Wendy said it freaked her out a bit because my jaw was completely over to the other side of my mouth. It's like having one corner of your mouth touching the other corner of your mouth. Obviously, they hadn't been able to fix the broken jaw yet.

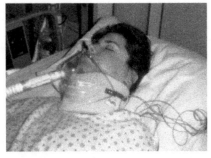

Me in ER bed with neck collar

They both stayed at the hospital with me the entire week that I was at Scottsdale Memorial. They stayed with Willa, my aunt's mother. Either Willa or Eileen drove Wendy and Mom to the hospital every day.

During the week at the hospital, they found out how I was admitted and the diagnosis of all my injuries.

Upon arriving at the hospital, I was admitted with level 1 head trauma with a Glasgow coma score of ten, which is a very intense-rated coma, acute concussion, and mandibular (jaw) fracture. They had placed me in a neck brace, as a C-spine precaution situation, with an IV and nasal tubes in place for oxygen. I was moaning constantly and didn't respond appropriately to voices. They found a laceration of my lower mandible. On the right side of my mouth, a few teeth had been chipped off at the upper back portion of the jaw. An upper right incisor was missing. My arms had to be restrained, due to the combativeness I came in with. A large laceration over the left knee was also found, and abrasions were noted at the left ankle area.

In the emergency room, X-rays were taken of my neck and chest. A Foley catheter was put in place for urination and I was taken to have a CAT scan for further evaluation. Upon looking at the CAT scan, it apparently showed a small amount of intracranial bleeding. I was intubated, which meant that I had a small tube placed into my throat, where my tooth was missing for feeding purposes. I was sedated prior to going into the CAT scan. After the scan, I remained unresponsive. I had gone into a coma. They then decided to admit me to the ICU, under the care of Dr. McFarland. Also, doctors Deen and Guyette were responsible for treating my mandibular fractures.

The next day, November 26, 1989, I underwent surgery on my jaw. They said I continued to improve over the next few days. I was slowly coming out of the coma and got to a point where I was awake, alert, and able to follow commands readily without obvious gross neurological deficits. My emotions remained easily altered, unstable, and I remained quite impulsive in my behavior. I wasn't fully oriented with place or time, but was making more sense with statements I made. They did a second head CAT scan on November 28 that showed the intracranial contents were back to normal. I was tolerating a good full liquid diet at that time. They felt they could transfer me to a rehab facility on December 6, 1989, where I was then placed into Meridian Point Rehabilitation Facility. There they placed me on an intensive program of occupational and physical therapy. My diet was to remain liquid because my jaw had been wired shut and a set of braces placed on both the top and lower jaws. I was being fed through a tube or a straw where the missing tooth had been broken off. I was glad later to find out, that I didn't have to have a feeding tube placed into my throat.

An evaluation of my situation was done on December 7. I was alert, cooperative and able to speak clearly and respond to questions. I was disoriented to where I was, but was aware of the month, date and who I was. I was able to stand and walk on my own with minimal assistance. I had some slight coordination problems when walking within my room, which was because I wasn't wearing my contacts.

In the cognition portion, they found that I appeared to be searching for answers to questions, but could eventually answer them correctly. I presented with a flat affect, (which is the absence or near absence of emotional response to a situation that normally elicits emotion) confused conversation, and demonstrated impairments in short-term memory.

On my body, I still had a wound on the left knee and a large two-inch diameter wound over the left ankle and my right leg had multiple scratches and bruises.

The assessment for me after the traumatic brain injury stated that I was presenting with confusion, impaired memory, and balance impairments. I only needed minimal assistance with transfers and gait. Which means, getting up from a seated position or vice versa and when trying to walk.

The short-term goals were to increase orientation of my surroundings, reduce my confusion, and improve my standing equilibrium, with the help of increasing strength balance in the left ankle.

The long-term goals were to increase walking on all terrain, return to my previous lifestyle, and to continue strengthening and endurance training in a community basis. I was to be seen individually, for physical therapy daily and be involved in groups for balance and leg strengthening and endurance exercises.

CHAPTER 8

My First Memories

When I came out of the coma, I had the mental age of a three-year-old and a terrible short-term memory. The portion of my brain that had been affected the most had to do with anger. I was combative and hard to restrain for a while.

The first memories that I had were more like foggy dreams. I wasn't sure for a long time if they were real or if I was dreaming. I felt very out of place and unsure of what was happening to me. I kept waking up in a hospital room with all these hoses and attachments hooked into me. I would see doctors just walking around and no one talking to me, like I wasn't really there. Conversations were about me, but I wasn't included. I couldn't respond even if I wanted to. All I could do was just lie there. I felt like I was watching someone else's life.

I have faint memories of the hospital at Scottsdale. The first real memories, I knew were mine, were of Meridian Point Rehabilitation Hospital in Scottsdale, Arizona. I remember being put into a room next to the nurses' station. It had a TV, bed, and bathroom that I couldn't initially use. A small table was placed in the room to put my flowers on and use as needed. There was one window on the right side of my bed that looked out onto the desert where there were palm trees. I was in a gown with my mouth wired shut, braces, and a brace around my left knee to keep it protected. I also had to wear a neck brace for a while. I had diapers, a bedpan at one point, and sponge baths. I was embarrassed at first, when I found out this information.

I was told on December seventh, that I had a hallucination where I was telling everyone that I was being held hostage in the hospital and wanted to leave, but they wouldn't let me. That night, I had proceeded to get out of my room and started to crawl down the hallway.

I was crawling due to the stitches they had placed in my left knee from the impact explosion of my left kneecap. I lost a lot of the cartilage in the knee and it was very weak.

Pulling myself down the hallway, I proceeded to pull out all the stitches in my knee and bled all over the carpet in the hall. One nurse found me, of course, and asked me where I was going. My understanding is I was trying to get back home to my family. I was being held there against my will and there was nothing wrong with me. I told her this, numerous times. She got the other nurses and some of the help on hand, to get me back to my room and put me into a straitjacket. This way, I couldn't hurt myself anymore and would be easier to handle, until I was thinking more clearly.

The next day, I was eating my breakfast in the mess hall and I watched my bed being taken out of my room. They placed mats on the floor, all the way around the room. Later I found out this was called a Craig Bed. After breakfast was done, they placed me back in the room, in my very safe environment. It's what I now call, my "rubber room." The mats were like ones from the gym at school. They were rubber, but soft so you can't hurt yourself. I was still in my straitjacket for a while.

I think it was about a week later that I eventually graduated out of the Craig Bed, to a regular bed again.

The nurses had patched my knee, the best they could, due to my antics being done on a weekend, when all the doctors were gone. I kept having the patch replaced for about one or two weeks. It was starting to heal on its own. They told me that I was supposed to have surgery to have it sewn back up again and that the longer we had to wait, the more it would hurt to fix it. I wanted to have it fixed, so I would continually ask when it was going to be done. The doctor who needed to do it was either too booked, on vacation, or something. I think my dressings had to be changed two to three times every day so it would not get infected.

I remember not liking the "rubber room" very much. I felt like I was in some crazy place, that didn't make any sense to me.

I kept thinking, "I didn't do anything wrong." I cried a lot, not being able to understand much of what was going on. All I knew was, my body hurt, I was missing something, and where were my clothes?

As time passed, I became a little more coherent and things were getting a little easier. Soon, I was able to get out of the straitjacket, but I was still in the "rubber room."

"How much longer...do I have to stay in this?" I asked one of the nurses.

"You'll have to stay in this room until we're sure that you won't try to go down the hallway again and tear up your knee any more than it already is." She turned and walked out of my room.

I only had a few visitors who would come to see me. They were my mom and my two sisters. No one else was able to see me at this point; but it was for reasons I wasn't aware of yet.

I remember a lot of just lying in bed and watching TV. I would be looking out my window in December and wondering why there wasn't any snow. I called my family and friends in Alaska telling them I was in a place that was holding me hostage and wouldn't let me out. I wanted them to come pick me up and take me home. Occasionally, I'd ask where Bruce was. He was my boyfriend in high school, and I still thought that was where I should be, in Alaska, with my boyfriend and why was I in a hospital that had palm trees?

Me in hospital room missing tooth

I eventually got my regular bed back and was able to sleep, off the floor. I was still eating with a straw at this point. My mouth had been wired shut with braces to keep my teeth from all falling out. There were three major breaks so that I almost had to have dentures at the age of nineteen. I had shakes for breakfast, lunch, and dinner. I drank through a straw where my front right eyetooth had been broken off upon impact. It wasn't very satisfying to only be able to drink your meals. After about two weeks of this, I lost my appetite for food. I only drank the shakes because they made me do it for nutrition. They would tell me that I needed to do it in order to heal properly. I didn't even get to go out to the commons area, where everyone else ate for a while. They didn't want me out of bed unless absolutely necessary.

Soon I was put into classes to start learning everything over again. I had such an impact to my head, when I hit the ground at the accident, that I had lost all my short-term memory. I couldn't make a sentence; most of the time I kept on forgetting what I wanted to say. Then someone would have to put me back on track again, to finish what I started to say or ask. It was very frustrating. I used to have such a good memory back in high school. Now it's all but gone. I'd have to learn most everything all over again.

They started me out with shapes and matching them up to holes that the shape would fit into. It took awhile just to get those down, but I was a fast learner. A young man who was in college studying rehabilitation was assigned to help me out with getting to my classes and back. I don't remember his name, but he talked with me and helped me out a lot during this time of need, pushing me in a wheelchair, to and from my room and checking me in and out of classes.

The day finally came when they were going to stitch my knee back up. I was glad but afraid at the same time, because I knew this was going to hurt, A LOT! The wound had started to heal around the edges, making the skin tight and scabbed over. They had tried to keep the knee as soft as possible for as long as possible, just so that the skin wouldn't try to heal so quickly. What can I say? I'm a fast healer. I was taken back to the hospital and had surgery on the knee. When they brought me back to Meridian Point, I was heavily sedated and given a morphine drip button to use, if the pain got too bad. I was in so much pain after the surgery that I was trying to give myself more than what the drip would let me have in an hour's timeframe.

My mom, sister Wendy, and Ralph and Lavonne Ertz, friends from Alaska who were traveling through Arizona, came to see me after I had gotten back to my room. I don't remember much of their visit, being in and out of consciousness due to the drugs. I remember them talking to me and constantly asking how I was feeling. I remember telling them how much pain I was in and asking for more drugs. I would give myself a shot of the morphine and then pass out for half an hour or so, then wake up and try it again. The drip only let you take a hit so many times in a given period. My visitors all prayed for me and one even gave me a foot massage, trying to ease my pain. The thought was nice, but it didn't help much. I was in agony for a good forty-eight hours after the surgery.

Once things started to calm down with my knee, the nurses came into my room and gave me a leg brace that went all the way up to my groin and down to my ankle with a hole at the knee so I couldn't bend my leg. I wore that for the next six weeks to let the knee heal during my rehab. It also kept me from walking on it and put me in a wheelchair.

As time went by, I started to really show some great improvements. The doctors were all very impressed at how fast I was picking things back up and able to hold conversations without too much difficulty. I even had nurses on the late shifts come in and talk with me during the night. They said they were bored and I was good company compared to a lot of the other patients in the hospital. My back hurt a lot as well, but they said it wasn't broken. Due to the pain I was in at night, I got a lot of back massages during those conversations. They helped me out a lot. It didn't cure the problem, but it sure made me relax a little more.

A lot of the patients in the hospital were way worse off than I was and never getting out. Some had head injuries that left them without speech and in very foul moods most of the time. Some had no control over their bodily functions or were very loud with constant uncontrollable noises. I felt very bad for a lot of the residents who were in the facility. I didn't feel like I was that bad and shouldn't have been taking up a room for someone who did need it, but they wouldn't let me leave. I had to put my time in.

I remember the first time I was able to get up out of my bed and go to the bathroom, on my own. It was a great feeling not to have to worry about bedpans or being washed up by someone else. I went into the bathroom, in my wheelchair, and looked into the mirror. I about screamed but couldn't. I was stunned and confused. I didn't recognize the person who I saw in the mirror at all. I thought my brain had been taken out of my body and put into someone else's. I looked terrible. My hair was long and straight and looked like a mess. I had huge glasses on, since they wouldn't let me wear my contacts. I saw what I looked like with braces and my mouth wired shut. I also had lost quite a bit of weight with this whole ordeal. It's very degrading to see yourself in this manner and not understand what has happened to you and why or how this transpired. With my jaw being broken then reset, I had a new jawline that made it look more squared off rather than oval like before the accident. It was going to be a whole new me, after this one. It was very confusing to be in this type of situation. I honestly didn't know what to think. All I knew was that I wanted to go home, to a more familiar place.

After coming out of the bathroom I remember wondering, exactly what did really happen to me? I had no idea what I'd been through and no one was talking about it.

For the next one to two weeks, I was put on a rigorous schedule of learning. I had a neurological class, a reading and writing class, and a physical therapy class. I'm sure there were more classes than this, but these were my major ones that stuck out.

The nurses and doctors were very impressed at the rate of improvement I was making. They said, they could see improvements on a daily basis. I thought this was great and that I would be going home sooner, if I did well.

It was about this time that I started asking more questions about what had happened to me. I was surprised that Jason hadn't come to see me yet, but I also didn't want him to see me in the situation I was in either. I didn't ask too many questions, just due to that line of thinking. I just figured that he was busy with the full-time work hours and he wanted me to get better and would see me when they thought it was best. Or maybe he knew what I did to get into this situation and was just too embarrassed to come see me. I figured that I got into a fight or something and got my butt kicked.

About a week before Christmas, just before my mom and younger sister were about to head back home, I was told there was going to be a meeting with the doctor in his office. I started to get excited. I thought for sure they were going to tell me that I was well enough to head home.

I was getting ready to see all my friends and Jason again. I couldn't wait for this!

We all went into the doctor's office and sat down. The meeting involved the doctor, my sisters, my mother, and me. The doctor proceeded to ask me lots of questions about how I was doing and how I felt, trying to see where I was mentally and physically. After about a half dozen questions, he sat up in his chair and leaned forward, while resting his arms and hands on his desk in front of himself.

"Okay, I think she's ready to hear it now. I'm confident that she can handle the situation. Go ahead and tell her." He then sat back in his chair and rested his arms across his chest, watching intently.

I looked over at my mom and sisters with a big grin and said, "Do I get to go home now?"

Just as I asked the question, both my sisters started to cry.

My mom looked at me. "Do you remember what happened in your accident?"

"No, I just know I was in some kind of accident or fight and now I'm getting better." I started to wonder if there was something else wrong with me.

"Chery...Jason didn't make it." Mom started to cry.

I looked at them and just shook my head. "That's not even funny."

"No Chery, Jason was in the accident with you and he didn't make it. He died at the scene," Dawn said to me.

The first words out of my mouth are ones that no parent ever wants to hear their child say. I had a look of disbelief on my face when I said, "I wish I were dead." I got angry. I had so many different emotions running through my head. I didn't know which way was up.

"Oh no!" my mom exclaimed, grasping one hand over her mouth and starting to cry even harder.

Pointing to me, the doctor said, "That's exactly why we couldn't tell her any sooner than this. We had to wait to make sure she'd be able to handle the information and her body wouldn't just go into shutdown phase. She's going to need a lot more attention while she goes through this stage in the healing process. You can take her back to her room now." He dismissed us from his office.

My mind was reeling from the information I'd just gotten. I went from being in a hopeful and excited situation, to the worst possible information a person can get. Now I understood why Jason hadn't come to see me. I wondered why he had died and not me. Who else was at the scene and had information I needed? What was going to happen to me now? The worst thing of all was the fact that I couldn't even remember what happened to us both.

They wheeled me back to my room and we are all crying by now. I wanted to know so desperately what had happened.

"Why won't anyone tell me what happened?" I said very loudly and sternly.

"Well, all we know is that you were hit by a drunk driver while you, Jason, Joe, and Christy were out riding three-wheelers. We called the Robbe family and Joe to let them know that you were getting the news today. They should be here shortly," my mom said, between tears.

Dawn said, "I knew something was up when I didn't hear from you and Jason. You guys were supposed to pick me up for the big class reunion party that you helped put together, remember? When I didn't get the call from you, I started getting worried that you forgot about me. I made a phone call over to his house and no one had heard from you guys, which we all thought was weird, knowing the big plans that you both had for that evening," she said.

CHAPTER 9

The Explanation

Shortly after that the Robbe family, Joe, Christy, and my roommate Eileen showed up in my room. I remember sitting in a chair, on the opposite side of the room from the window not doing really well and still trying to believe what I'd been told. Looking down, I was wondering what's going to happen to me now? We had such big plans that we were working on with his invention and possibly moving in together or getting married. I just couldn't get over it. It kept repeating itself over and over in my mind. It felt like a tape being played, on a constant loop.

When I finally looked up, Joe and Renee were walking toward me. Renee asked, "Chery, are you okay?"

"No Renee, they just told me that Jason is dead. Is...is that true?" I said with tears and sniffles, waiting for her to tell me that he was just fine.

"Yes." Renee started to cry as well. "He didn't make it. Do you remember what happened?"

"I remember ...Joe, Christy, Jason, and I going out riding in the desert. We had a blast and came home that night for a party with my friends from Alaska. I don't remember what happened with the party though," I answered, with some hesitation and confusion. It didn't make sense to me, unless I had too much to drink or something. I looked up at Renee, waiting for affirmation on what I had just told her.

"Well, that's partially right," she said. She looked over at Joe and Christy, who were hugging each other, waiting for the story to be told. "You did go out riding with them, but you never made it home. Joe, why don't you go over what happened with her?" She backed away from me slowly, to let Joe have some room, and went over to where he was standing with Christy.

Joe slowly walked over to me. I was still sitting in my chair. I don't think I would have been standing after what he told me next.

Wondering what I was actually going to remember, Joe started asking me questions.

"Chery, do you remember going out to the wash area and riding the three-wheelers?" he asked.

"Yes, I remember that."

"Do you remember talking about taking the last trip out, before returning home for your party?"

"Yes, Jason and I had a long discussion about the better helmet and who was going to wear it, in case something happened," I said.

"Yeah. Well, it wouldn't have mattered with him if he had been wearing the helmet," he said quietly and starting to tear up again.

"TELL ME WHAT HAPPENED ALREADY!" I yelled. I wanted to know the truth. I looked around the room at everyone, then back at Joe.

"On that last trip out, we took the one trail that we hadn't been on yet. I was in front of both of you and my machine stopped; it just quit for no reason. It was weird. Do you remember that?"

I bent my head down as if to think deeply and remember what I could. "Yes, I remember that. I told Jason to wait for you or to go back and to help you figure out what was wrong with your machine. We turned around and went back to where you were already fiddling around with the choke. I remember something about you guys taking the dipstick and rubbing it around in the dirt and then putting it back in to get it started." Having a confused look on my face, I looked back up at Joe. "I thought that was very weird, by the way. I was really sure we weren't going to get your machine started again after that." Then I looked down at the floor again and continued on with what was next. "I remember your machine started back up. You and Jason high-fived each other and Jason got back on the machine with me. He put our machine in gear and took off. I remember seeing you get on your machine and slowly start behind us. I turned back to look straight ahead and there was a wall of stone with a sharp 90-degree corner to the right. On the wall of stone in front of us, someone had painted 'I LOVE JASON' in white lettering. The love part was replaced with a big heart instead."

A smile came over me, as I remembered that part. "We both thought it was funny. We looked at each other and said, 'I love you.' After that, we went back to the car and headed home." I looked up again at Joe. His eyes were tearing up, but he was holding back the tears the best he knew how. "That's what I remember. I mean, I don't know how all this happened to me." I pointed to myself, with the knee issue and my jaw wired shut. "I guess I must have gotten into a fight at the party. Or maybe I made Eileen mad and we got into it," I said jokingly and looking at Eileen with a grin.

"I don't think it would have been you in this hospital room if we had gotten into a fight. I'd be the one lying in bed in agony, not you," Eileen piped in saying in a joking but serious voice. "I don't think I could compete with your karate skills. I'd probably be in worse shape than you." That was kind of an icebreaker for what was about to happen. The mood, for a very short term, was a little lighter. Then it went back to Joe.

As he leaned in toward me, he said, "Well, you seemed to remember most of what happened. Think about right after you saw the words on the wall. Do you remember what happened next?" Waiting intently to hear what I would say.

"We went back to the car." In my mind, I had finished off the day with a very happy ending, but that was not what really happened.

"Chery, you both never made it back to the car." Then Joe said very carefully, "I want you to listen to what I have to say before you say anything else, okay?" He had taken my hand and held onto it tightly.

I had a confused look on my face. "Okay," I said, not really sure I should be agreeing to this.

"After we got going again, you both started into the corner. I don't think any of us heard or saw what was coming next. A GMC step-side pickup truck came hauling around the corner, and hit you both head-on. The police estimated that he was doing about fifty miles per hour when he hit you." Joe stopped for just a moment to make sure I was okay and able to take this all in. He looked at me with a questioning stare and I nodded back at him to continue.

"When the truck hit you, it crushed Jason's chest and he died instantly. They said he probably never even knew what hit him. It threw you back about fifteen feet and you landed headfirst on the ground, smashing that top of the line helmet you both were fighting over, just a little while earlier." Joe stopped again to check on me. This time, I was tearing up pretty good. I had a pretty good hold on his hand. I nodded again.

Joe continued, "I had to get out of the way, before he hit me and dove into the trees with my machine. Jason had fallen off to the right side of the machine and you were lying on the ground a ways back. The truck continued to drive over the top of the three-wheeler before stopping. He had to back his truck off the machine to get free." We were both in tears pretty well, at this point. "I screamed at the top of my lungs, not believing what I'd just seen," Joe said, with tears rolling down his cheeks.

I didn't know what to say. I was so heartbroken and full of tears, confusion, rage, and disbelief. My life had just made one of the biggest changes I would ever know. The future I was looking forward to had just vanished. All I wanted to do was get my hands on the driver of that vehicle. Little did I know there was still more to this story that I hadn't yet learned.

"WHY?" It's all I could ask, say, or even mutter after that. I couldn't comprehend why the day we were having so much fun and was going so well could end so badly. All I could do was just cry. Everyone in the room took turns trying to console me, but without any luck. Soon, it was time for everyone to go home. I was left alone in my hospital room with only memories of what I had with Jason. I was trying so hard to finish that day in my head with thoughts of the things we were planning to do together and what kind of life we would have had. I was crushed. My heart, I swear, felt like someone had taken a dull knife to it and ripped it in two.

The next day, the distraught Robbe family came by my hospital room. They had brought me the Christmas items that Jason had bought for me. I guess they thought I would like to have them with me, rather than at their house.

"I know it's not quite Christmas yet, but with just finding out about Jason, we wanted to comfort you the best we could. We thought having these items might help." They proceeded to give me the few things that he'd purchased for me. Some were already wrapped and some weren't.

Martha said, "Jay's favorite holiday was Christmas. He always loved getting things for other people." She smiled. They proceeded to help me put up the neon clock on my wall and found other spots in my room for the other gifts.

"I want to go to the funeral. When is it?" I asked, impatiently.

It was quiet at first. Nobody knew what to say. Everyone just looked around at each other. Then I heard, "Chery, the funeral was last month. We couldn't wait to have it with you because we didn't know how long you were going to be in a coma," said Martha.

"Great! So I missed that too! Awesome! When do I get a break on this?" I asked, sarcastically and upset, throwing my arms up in the air. "I didn't even get to say my good-byes."

I asked, "Has anyone seen the ring that Jason gave me?"

Martha asked, "What ring are you talking about, my dear?"

"The ring that I got from Jason. It was his ring. It was a pinkie ring that fit my ring finger perfectly on my right hand. I was wearing it when we went out that day. I never took it off. He told me it was a promise ring. I miss it and would like to wear it, if I can. Do they have it behind the counter?" I asked, hopefully that someone would be able to bring it right in to me.

"I'll go ask, but nobody has said anything to us about a ring that I know of," she said, and started out of the room toward the nurses' station. After I had a few minutes of conversation with Jason's dad and sisters, Martha walks back in. "The front desk said they have a bag of your stuff that was taken off you at the scene and will bring it to you in just a bit. They need to locate it first," she replied with a smile.

Soon, the nurse returned with a bag of items that were mine. I went through everything in it. I found no ring. I did, however, come across the pants that Eileen let me wear. They were cut from top to bottom on both sides of the legs, to get them off me. I knew I'd have some serious apologizing to do after that one. I'd have to take her shopping to get a new pair.

"Out of all the items in here, I can't find the one thing I really wanted. The ring," I said, sadly and disappointed. I put everything back in the bag and set it on the floor. I got back into bed and crawled under the covers to get away from it all.

"Maybe after church, a couple of us can run back out to the site and see if we can find it on the ground," Renee said, hopefully. "It may have just fallen off upon the impact or something."

"Thanks, Renee. I'd really appreciate that. That ring is the last thing I have that he was able to give me himself. It's more special now, than it was when he gave it to me the first time," I said.

At that point, Martha chimed in. "Do you know what Jason was planning on doing for Christmas this year?" She was looking right at me, as she was asking the question.

"Well, not really. I guess spending it with you guys. I wanted him to come home with me to Alaska for Christmas so he could meet my family. He said he didn't have enough money for a plane ticket," I said sadly. "Now, I guess that will never happen."

Martha just stood there looking at me. Then she spoke, "Well, there's more to that story than you know Chery. Jay didn't want you to know that he'd already bought a ticket to go with you. He was planning on surprising you to be able to go back and ask your mom a question."

"What question?"

All I could do is just wait for the answer that I was hoping was going to come out of her mouth, but at the same time was terrified to hear.

"He wanted to ask your mom for your hand in marriage," she said, almost in tears. "He has had this planned out for a while. He was going to take the trip with you, get the okay from your family, then plan the wedding to happen here this summer," she said.

I was stunned. I didn't even know what to say. I kept thinking, I was going to get married, but now I can't. How unfair is that? All I could do, in an outburst, was just cry. All I wanted to do was just hold him and say, yes! I couldn't even do that. I never got to have that awesome moment with him. My heart again felt like it was crushed.

Renee walked over to me, and as she bent over to hug me she said, "He loved you so much. All the other girls he dated were nothing like you. All they wanted him for was what he could give them, or just for looking good with him and riding around in a nice car. Some just wanted to party all the time. You were different. He liked not having to feel like he needed to impress you all the time. He didn't need to live up to any expectations. You liked him, just for the person he was. No more, no less. Even after you found out about his past, you stuck with him trying to help him do the right thing. Not many girls I know, who knew him, were like that. In fact, I don't know any." Renee kind of gives off a slight giggle and looks around the room at her family, who also do the same.

After a sniffle and swallow, I said, "Thank you. I needed to hear that. I was never really sure how I fit in, with all the other friends he had. The girls were all so sassy and beautiful. The guys were all like jocks from school. I never fit into that crowd. I wasn't comfortable, but I liked everyone. I kept thinking that at some point he'd get tired of me. I was too boring for him or something. My idea of fun was different than his, but we always had a good time when we went out."

"Oh my dear, you're the one who kept him from having something else happen to him before this," replied his mom, as she came up to hug me as well. "I was always so afraid that I'd get a phone call telling me that he'd been shot or in a wreck of some sort. You made him think twice about what he was doing. Even though he may have never said anything to you, it was always you, who he was thinking about."

"While I was going through Jay's room, I was cleaning out the drawers under his water bed. I found a letter that had been written only a few days before your trip," Renee said, as she was pulling the letter out of her pocket. "It almost sounds like he...that Jason knew something was going to happen to him." She handed the letter to me and I read through it slowly, so as to take in every word and understand where he was coming from. He thanked his mom and dad for everything they had done in his life so far and much bigger things were on the horizon for him. Renee asked, "Do you remember him writing this? Were you even with him when he did?"

"No, I wasn't with him and I have no idea when he wrote it. This is the first I've ever seen or heard of it, at least, from what I can remember anyway." I knew that I very easily could have been with him, but can't remember due to memory loss. I still don't think I was with him on that day though. I wanted to include the letter in this story, but no one has been able to find the letter since.

All I could do was just cry and think about how I was supposed to be getting married. Now, due to the recklessness of someone else, it would not happen. I didn't want to believe that the last couple of days had even happened. It was so much to take in, at one time. I didn't want it to be true, but deep down I knew that it was, which made it even harder to swallow. It was a very surreal time for me. The end of visiting hours came and everyone went back home. I, again, was left alone to handle this new information, all by myself. I was starting to wonder if it was even worth being around for. I didn't know how much more I could take. I was starting to lose faith in everything and everyone.

During all of this, somehow Sam Meranto had gotten word that Jason and I had been in an accident. Sam had a TV show and Jason was a guest. His show helped you beat bad habits. He got hold of me in the hospital to see how I was doing. We spoke on the phone for a short time. Meanwhile, he was trying to figure out where I was mentally. He said that he was going to make me some tapes that would help me heal faster and deal with all the grief I had just been through. He asked if I would listen to the tapes and not just ignore them. I said that I would listen. After all, I didn't have anything else I was going to be doing for a while.

I think it was just a couple days after that, when he stopped by the hospital and talked with me for a good amount of time. He dropped off the tapes and said that if I used them, they would help me get back on my feet faster. God is good at working in mysterious ways.

I thanked him and listened to the tapes every night after that.

CHAPTER 10

Christmas

My mom and sister Wendy had to fly back to Alaska. They had been in Arizona for almost a month and had to get back to their regular lives. It was almost Christmas and I wasn't sure how I was going to be spending it this year.

Before my mom left, the doctor had talked with her, my two sisters, and me in my room. The doctor said that I was going to have to be careful about how my emotions were handled. The part of my brain that had been injured in the accident was the one that controls anger and frustration. He said I would have to learn how to handle my anger and hold in what didn't need to be said. At this point, if I had something to say, I would just let it out. It didn't matter if it was good or bad; it just came out. I also needed help on what words to use to express myself. That would be tricky for me, for a while. If anyone made me mad, I'd just let him have it. I didn't even care what the outcome was, especially with everything that had happened.

All I had was time on my hands these days. I did the good girl thing and followed my daily schedule. Getting up, eating, going to the scheduled classes, and just spending the rest of my time in my room, thinking about all that had happened in this past week. What does it all mean? Where do I go from here? What happens to me now? Do I just go back home or try to stay and work things out here? I really want to go back to my job, but will they look at me the same ever again? Can I even do the job I had before, with my memory problems? It was just question after question running through my head. It was tiring me out. It's been so long since I've been in here; maybe Eileen even got a new roommate. Nothing is certain. All sense of security is gone. It's Christmas Eve and I have no way of knowing what to do next. I'm alone in my room, silent.

The next morning, I woke up to cheering in the hallways. "Merry Christmas!" is what I heard. I got out of bed and fixed myself up in the bathroom, before making my way out to the main lobby, where everyone gathered to eat and watch TV. Lots of the other patients had family there to celebrate Christmas with. Some however did not, so the nurses and helpers kept them all busy doing projects, so they would also feel included in the festivities. I just stayed next to the nurses' station and watched.

"Good morning Chery," said, one of the nurses behind the glass window. "I have a message for you." She reached down and picked up a message from the Robbe family from about thirty minutes earlier. "They said they'll be by in about an hour, so if you want to have breakfast, now would be a good time," she suggested.

I looked down at the piece of paper. It said exactly what she told me. I knew there wasn't much time before they got there, so I ate breakfast and finished just as they had arrived. It was so busy in the lobby area that we decided to all go out in back and sit around one of the tables outside to visit. I was still being pushed around in a wheelchair, if I was outside the facility. I remember being wheeled through the entire facility with the Robbe family and going out the back doors, where it was much quieter. It was a very sunny day, with a bright blue sky. The temperature was in the low seventies and very comfortable. This was not at all what I was used to for Christmas, but it was nice just the same.

Martha asked, "So Chery, how have you been doing, since learning everything?"

With a big sigh, I replied, "I don't really know. I've just been following my normal routine as much as I can. I try to stay busy because when I'm by myself I think about Jason. Actually, I thought I'd be in Alaska right now. I'm not really sure how to handle Christmas in the desert," I said with a smile. "How was your morning with the family? I mean, did you guys do anything for Christmas morning?" I asked, trying to lighten the mood and to change the direction of the conversation.

"No, we just got up and had breakfast," laughed Renee. "We knew we'd be coming here to be with you, so we didn't make any plans."

"Thank you," I said, as I started to cry. "I'm so glad that you came to see me today. With my mom and Wendy gone back home and Dawn having her commitment this morning I wasn't sure what I was going to do today. I mean I knew I'd probably see everyone; I just didn't know when." Then there was silence. I cried a little harder and just lost it. "I miss Jason!"

Renee gave me a big hug and said, "I know; we all do."

"It's going to be different now that he's not here to give all those wise cracks that he always came up with," said Martha, thinking about the fun times at Christmas. "He loved Christmas. It was his favorite holiday. He looked forward to this all year and now...now, I just don't know what I'm going to think about it," she said, sobbing.

We all sat and consoled each other for some time, while talking and remembering Jason and the things he did or said. Well, time flies when you're going through old memories and it was starting to get late.

"We should probably get you back to your room, before they think we kidnapped you or something. We need to be heading back home as well," said Martha. Starting to tear up, she looked around at everyone. She asked me, "When are they supposed to let you out of here?"

"I don't know. I think soon, but they want to make sure I can do things on my own before then. I heard someone talking about a rehabilitation facility that I may be going to first. I guess to try to get me back on my feet and to get into a routine again. I also heard about some gym training or something. I'll have to ask." I said this, feeling like I was never going to get out of that place.

On the way back to my room, we took an outside walk around the place. I showed everyone how I'd learned how to jump the sidewalks with my wheelchair and to pop a wheelie as well. I was getting pretty good learning new tricks, as more time went by.

They got me back to my room and everyone took turns giving me hugs and kisses and telling me they'd be by soon, to check on me again. Dawn was supposed to be by later that evening to see me, after the Christmas party she had gone to. I crawled back into bed and just lay there, relaxing for a bit. Again, I was alone.

I started to have thoughts running through my head all over again. Now what? Where do I go from here? Will I still have my job after I get out? When will I get out? Will I go live with Dawn when I'm done here? Do I just need to move back home? How would I do that by myself? The list went on and on. I was so overwhelmed by not having any kind of control of my life. I just decided to quit everything.

My room was empty. The sun was going down outside my window as I looked out, to see palm trees and sand.

"I can't do this by myself Jason. I don't want to do this by myself. I'm done! I'm just done!" I said, as I put my head in my hands and just started to cry as hard as I could. At that minute, I thought someone had heard me from the hallway and walked into my room. I felt two very warm and comforting arms wrap themselves around me, and just squeeze. Instantly, I felt no pain. I just stopped crying, almost like someone had turned off the faucet. It startled me and I wanted to see who had come into my room and made me feel so safe and secure. I looked up to see that my room was still empty. It made no sense to me. Were they in the bathroom?

"Hello?" I asked, trying to figure out where they'd gone. I got up out of bed and looked all around my room. No one was there, to be found. I hobbled out in to the lobby area and asked the nurse if someone had just come in or left my room.

"No one has entered or left your room since your friends brought you back earlier," she replied, a little confused.

"Okay, thank you," I said, as I turned away from her.

I hobbled back into my room with crutches and sat back on my bed. I was thinking to myself; I think I was just touched by Jason or God or something. I went back through the entire thing in my head. I know that with nobody else being in the room, I had to have been touched by God in that moment. Never in my life, had I felt so much peace and so instantly. I couldn't have cried if I wanted to, and I tried. I understood, at that point, that I'd been left here for a reason and everything was going to be fine. I knew that Jason was in a much better place and was still looking out for me, even through all this. This enlightenment will stick with me for the rest of my life. No one will ever be able to tell me that there is no God or heaven! I know because I got to witness it. After this experience, I began to look at things a little more differently. I knew I would get to see Jason again. It's just a matter of time and patience.

Dawn came to see me later and I told her what happened. She didn't know what to say. Then she told me to call Mom, so I did. I told her what happened.

"Chery, I think you just got to experience something only a few people ever get to. You may think it was Jason, because he's the one you were calling out to. I think God himself touched you. Even if it was Jason, the only way that would have happened, is if God would have allowed it. The description that you gave, with the peace and tranquility you had, leads me to believe otherwise. Only one can give you that comfort. WOW!" she said. We finished our phone call and by that time, it was getting pretty late. Dawn went back home and I felt better about being in my room that night. I wasn't so alone anymore.

CHAPTER 11

Rehabilitation

I had a lot of hard work ahead of me, to get back the life that I was going to be leading. I was still having a hard time completing some sentences, forgetting what I was going to say, and losing my train of thought about what the conversation was all about. I had to really start working on retraining my mind. It seemed that things that didn't have as much interest were harder to retain or stay on track with. If I had a good solid foundation for a subject, it would not be as hard to follow.

As I was starting to get better, I learned that Chris Robbe had seen her doctor again. I wasn't sure why at first, but then I found out. The cancer she'd had as a child, had returned. They weren't sure how bad it was going to be. I would be praying for her as well.

After learning how to put blocks into holes, with the same shapes, and learning how to read and write all over again, I was starting to feel like I could really get back out into the real world and start living again.

I went and got my braces off in January of 1990. They took the wiring out and started to talk about getting an implant for where my tooth had been knocked out, in front. I thought that I'd be back doing my old routine soon, but they said I still had one more phase I had to go through—assisted living, to get me ready to enter back into my own life.

After completing the rehabilitation at Meridian Point, I had to go to an assisted living facility to learn how to cook and clean and take care of myself before they would let me back into my own place.

I remember taking everything down in my room that was on the walls and shelves. It was a lot, since I had been there for so long. I had accumulated a few pictures of Tom Cruise because they were so similar to pictures I had of Jason. I packed up and went over to my new temporary living quarters. It was more like an apartment complex that had a few rented spots, for people like me. I think it was in Scottsdale, but I can't remember for sure. When I got to the place I was staying in, I had a sort of roommate already. He was a very nice man who was very rich and who had fallen off a horse and been paralyzed from the neck down. He was in a wheelchair that he could move around with his mouth. We never really talked much, because we didn't have anything in common. He was an older man, and I was a teenager who was missing someone I could only dream about now.

I unpacked my suitcase and placed the things from the hospital room in their new home for a while. It was a nice room, very spacious and clean. I had my own bathroom and walk-in closet, which I thought was very cool. When I was in my room, I could do whatever I wanted and the help would have to knock or ask if they could come in before just entering. It was nice to get some sort of privacy back. I put my pictures up on the wall next to my bed, and just sat on the queen-size bed, looking at them for the longest time. I wondered what my life would have been like, if Jason and I would have made it through the accident unharmed. Where would I be right now? Would we have been able to make it to some other event with big-name stars? We should have been in an apartment together already, getting ready for wedding plans. All I could do was pull myself into a tight ball and just cry on the bed.

Later that evening, my planner came over to help lay out what was expected of me, in this next portion of the rehabilitation stage. I remember being told I would need to come up with a grocery list for the month, on a low-income salary that contained foods that were to be cooked for everyone in the apartment and not just processed foods. They would need to be healthy and homemade dinners. I was in charge of the kitchen for one or two weeks at a time; I can't remember. Then my roommate's assistant would also have time to do the same. I was going to have a schedule to try to get myself back into a work mode. I would have a wake-up time, shower, and dress time, and to be out for breakfast in time, and to eat and clean up the kitchen, then brush my teeth and have some me-time before making it over to the gym that was just on the other side of the parking lot. I had a two-hour workout that was planned and set up for me. It was to get the muscle in my left leg back to where it was closer to my right leg, after wearing the brace for so long. I loved those workouts. I also got to walk over to my workouts with another girl who had joined recently and who lived across the path from me. Her name was Sandy. We got to be really good friends. After the workouts, I was to come back and take a shower, eat and/or prepare lunch, clean the kitchen, if it was my turn, and then do some memory exercises for about an hour or so. I had about an hour of free time afterward. Then it was time to prepare for dinner. After dinner, it was time to clean up the kitchen and to take the evening off to watch TV, or go to your room and do whatever you want. I spent a lot of time in my room listening to music, reading magazines, watching TV, and just thinking.

When I wasn't doing the required elements of my stay, I was in my room. I did a lot of soul-searching and "what-if" situations. It wasn't going to get me anywhere, but it did make me feel better. I had visitors on and off while I was there, but those visits also had time limits. I didn't have any type of transportation except my feet, to get me anywhere. All I wanted to do, was get back into my own life, without being told what to do or how long to do it.

Sandy and I had spent a lot of time together. We did all of our workouts at the same time and learned about what happened to each other that resulted in us being there. Sandy, however, didn't end up as well off as I did from her accident. She was also on an off-road vehicle and got into an accident where she hit her head really hard. She had some brain damage and had lost the partial use of one of her arms. Also, one leg didn't want to bend at the knee. She had to swing it around or limp most of the time. As we got more time together working out, she was making great progress. She also had some difficulty with putting words together and spoke very slowly. This also got better, as time went on. Sandy used to ride horses and do competitive riding. Her parents had a really nice ranch that she went to once in awhile. I got to see their place once, and really liked it. I thought they were rich. Sandy and I kept in touch, after I left the facility. We did things together that I never could have possibly imagined.

If I remember correctly, I spent all of January and part of February 1990, in the living facility, before getting back into an apartment in the same complex as my sister. Before I left the complex, I was able to go through my daily schedule without any reminders from anyone, make all the meals by myself and clean up and walk over to the gym and do a full workout; this was all done without being accompanied by anyone. I had finished all my dentistry and doctor appointments, including getting my contacts back. I was ready to try to start my life again.

When I left the complex, I went back to Nineteenth and Thunderbird, where I had originally lived when we first moved to Phoenix. I was comfortable there and knew my way around pretty well. They had a gym, pool, tennis courts, and pool tables in the commons area of the main house. So I was able to get the workouts that I needed to help regain the confidence and strength I required. My sister lived in the front of the complex and I lived in the back of the complex. It was an easier living situation for us both and she would give me rides to and from work.

The first thing I had to do was get new furniture. I had looked on the board at the office, and some people were moving out in the same complex and had a waterbed. I had never put one together or moved one before. After contacting the owners, I spoke with my coworkers and asked if anyone could help me get it over to my apartment. I had two or three guys say they would help on the weekend. The owners were okay with that. I then found some living room furniture and a kitchen table and chairs. The furniture was plush black with gold framework. We got the queen-size waterbed into the bedroom and set it up. Someone had brought over a hose to hook up in the bathroom to fill the bed. By the time that weekend was over, I had a very stylish apartment to live in.

I went back to work on March 1, 1990, at MCI and was really glad to see everyone again. I had some retraining, but remembered how to do the job pretty quickly. I worked in the residential verifications department, making sure that people who switched over from another company understood how everything worked with the switch. I had a lot of friends who took me under their wings and watched out for me.

One day during work, I wasn't feeling well and said I was going to the rest room to try to gather myself together. As I was coming back to my cubicle, I stopped, felt dizzy, and turned white. Everyone stopped what they were doing and looked at me.

My supervisor asked, "Chery, are you feeling okay?"

"I feel like I'm lightheaded and going to faint," I replied as I put my hands up to my face and went to sit in my chair.

She asked, "Are you having a seizure or something? Did they say this might happen?"

I replied, "Well, I was told, if I started to have any weird sensations or feelings that it could be something serious, and to just call my doctor's office so he can check the symptoms."

I took the phone number out of my purse and handed it over to her. She called my doctor and he put her through some questions about my situation and what had happened. He told her that it did sound like I had a seizure of some sort. They couldn't say if it would keep happening or not, but to just watch over me and keep them informed.

I had called down to my sister in her cubicle and told her what happened. She came up to my office and talked with me for a bit.

"Are you okay?" Dawn started out.

"I think I'm fine. I guess we'll just have to see if it happens again. Maybe I didn't eat enough or get enough sleep or something. I honestly don't know what would have caused this," I replied. I was sitting in my chair, just rubbing my neck and head.

"Well, the night is almost over. Maybe, you can go to bed early this evening and get some rest," my supervisor suggested.

One of my coworkers asked, "Now, with you being in your apartment alone, do you think that's safe? Do you need to have someone stay the night, just to make sure you don't have another episode during the night?"

"You don't even have a car," replied another coworker.

"I'm sure, I'll be fine," I said. "If I have a problem, I'll call Dawn. She's only two minutes from my place and has a car."

Dawn nodded her head to indicate that she was okay with this. "I'll call and check on her through the evening."

With that, everyone went back to work and the rest of the night went just fine.

I got a phone call a few days later from my attorney that he was taking a deposition from the driver of the truck that hit us, and wanted to know if I wanted to be there for it.

"Of course I do," I said.

"Now, if I let you sit in on this, you have to understand a few things. You can't say or do anything during this disposition. You can only be in the room as the victim of the accident. If you say anything or make a reaction of any kind, you will be asked to leave the room. Do you understand?"

"Yes," I said.

"I'm hoping that with you in the room, he'll be a little more uncomfortable and say something stupid. I, however, think that his attorney will take the Fifth on every question that we ask, for the most part. It's not going to be easy for you to do this, you know."

"Yeah, I know. I do want to know who this guy is though, and see if he can admit to his mistake. When is the deposition?"

"It'll be in two days. I'll give you directions and you can have someone just drop you off, or they can wait in the waiting room."

I asked, "Are any of the Robbe family going to be there for this?"

"I've called to invite them, but they have refused to be in the room. I don't think they can handle being with the guy. I sure hope you don't snap on me in there."

"I'll do my best to be on my best behavior."

The day finally came for the deposition and I managed to get a ride. My attorney again asked me if I was ready to do this. I told him that I needed to, more than anything. We proceeded into the room where there was a round table. If I remember correctly, there was the court reporter typing the entire deposition, the driver and his attorney, and my attorney with me. Just us five people going over this in one very small room. I was placed at the table close to the driver, but not right next to him. All I could do was just stare at him. My adrenaline was rushing through my body like a freight train. All I wanted to do was ask him, why? Even though we hadn't even started yet, I knew I couldn't say anything.

As we began the proceedings, the court reporter introduced herself and got everyone's names on record. I again was reminded that I couldn't say anything throughout the questioning. As the questions began, it was just like my attorney had said. One question after the next was answered with, "My client would like to plead the Fifth Amendment on this matter." Over and over, it was stated. I don't remember how long we were in the room, but it seemed like hours. I couldn't understand why he wouldn't just say what happened. Everyone who was there knows what he did. It's not like someone else was driving. Why can't he just admit to what he did? I think I would have had a little more respect for him, if he just would fess up to what he did, apologize, then we can get on with things. He would continue to deny that he was guilty for a long while after this.

As we spent our time listening to question after question, he wouldn't look at me or even lift his head up. He stared at the floor almost the entire time he was in the room. All I really wanted from him was to look up at me one time so I could look into his eyes and make him realize how much pain he was putting me through. Nope. He showed no expression on his face and appeared to be totally numb to the situation in the room. I think that is what made me more upset than anything.

After the proceedings were finished, he was escorted out by police. I left the room to release my frustrations and anger that had been steadily building up over time. I got very loud, and then just started crying.

"I told you this wasn't going to be easy," my attorney said as he handed me some tissues.

"I don't understand why he wouldn't let the guy answer any questions about what happened. He wouldn't let him say anything. Why?" I started to cry again.

"Well, the whole reason someone takes the Fifth, usually is to keep themselves from getting into more trouble than they are already in."

"Yeah, okay, but not even an apology for what he did?"

"That is an admission of guilt."

"He is guilty! We were there, we know what he did, how he did it, and I just want to know why he feels that he can do that and not have to answer for it!"

"Well, you're not going to get that answer today. You should have your ride take you home and try to not think about this deposition anymore. We're going to be working on this for a while longer, so it seems. If he keeps pleading that he's innocent, then we're in for a long journey ahead. Get some rest." He escorted me over to the door and let me out of the building. I went home and was very distraught for a few days after that, not being sure what was meant by the "long journey ahead."

CHAPTER 12

Things Were
Starting to Change

W hen I left the hospital, I had lost weight down to 115
pounds. I looked like a skeleton with skin. I almost
couldn't stand to look at myself in the mirror. I got down
to a pants size of seven and couldn't go any smaller due to the width of
my hips. I vowed that I would stay smaller, just with everything I'd been
through. It's amazing the attention you get, when you start looking a
little thinner.

Sandy and I did a few things together, after we left the rehab facility.
Her parents were very fond of the relationship we had made. Sandy had
been invited to a fundraiser for a rodeo show. She asked if I would come
along and help her out. I thought it sounded like a lot of fun.

When the weekend finally arrived, Sandy and her parents picked
me up at my apartment. We proceeded to the town it was held in. I

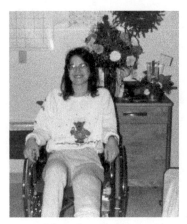

*Me in hospital room
just before I left*

Larry Wilcox with Sandy and me

can't remember the name of it offhand. I also didn't realize that a few celebrities would be in this rodeo. Sandy knew a lot of the people who were there, just from being in so many horse shows. She mixed and mingled with a lot of them. She would introduce me to some of them, we'd talk about what happened to the both of us, and everyone was so nice.

Then I saw him. It was Larry Wilcox, who played Officer Jon Baker on the TV show *Chips*. I use to watch the show all the time growing up. Larry was going to be riding in the competition today. I was so excited. We were introduced and had pictures taken with him and a few other riders. He was very nice and very handsome.

Since this was a fundraiser, there were a few people who wanted to talk with Sandy and I about another fundraiser that was going to be held, in the northern end of Phoenix. It was for concussions and trauma type injuries, the type we had sustained. We were invited to this, as guests. We accepted. Her parents said they would pick me up again. I greatly appreciated the hospitality they were showing me.

I went home that night in a very good mood and with some of my favorite pictures.

I went to work on Monday and told everyone about what had happened. One of my coworkers named Barbie suggested to me that since I lost all this weight, I should use it to my advantage and attempt to get some modeling jobs. She said most people diet forever trying to get to the size I was. The funny part about my situation was it had been so long since I was able to eat any solid foods that my body didn't crave food anymore. I could either eat as much as I wanted or nothing at all and I was fine. It's not exactly healthy to do that, but it worked. I could eat a whole pizza myself, which I did once to prove a point, or just not have anything at all. I knew it wouldn't last forever, but it was nice.

I didn't really take to heart the suggestion Barbie had about modeling. The way my childhood was, I didn't have much self-esteem for that kind of thing. I think that's one reason why I always wanted to be a screenwriter and never could really see myself in front of a camera, as an actress. I just didn't have the confidence that I looked good enough for that. I wondered later, if I should have at least tried it.

The night of the next fundraiser arrived. Sandy and her parents picked me up on their way to the location. We proceeded to the hotel, where the event was to play out. We were introduced to a lot of people there. One fellow in particular took a liking to me right away and started quite a long conversation with me. After the main portion of the event was over and dinner was finished, people had started to mix and mingle. I'm not going to give this person's name, but he was one of the stunt doubles for Roger Moore in the James Bond movies. He looked just like him. We sat down and talked about a lot of things that we both wanted in life, things we had done and things we still wanted to do. I was taken by his interest in me. The night ended on a good note. After some good evening pleasantries with the people I had met, Sandy's parents drove me home. They were asking a lot of questions about my conversation with the actor I mentioned earlier. Being the protective parents that they were, it was a good thing. Due to the age difference there was between us, they told me to be very careful and to look into his past more, before just continuing anything. I agreed.

The next day, I went to work. In the middle of the day, I had a delivery sent to my desk. It was a huge vase of roses!

The delivery person walked into the room. He asked, "I'm looking for a Chery. Is she here?"

"Those are for me?" I asked, both confused and curious. I had no idea who would be sending me flowers. "Who are they from?"

I took off my headset and got up from my chair as I took the flowers from the delivery person. He replied, "I don't know ma'am, but I don't usually get to deliver this size of vase. There's a card attached to the top. Maybe this will help you." He grabbed it off the top and handed it to me. "Admirer. You have someone interested in you, so it seems." The delivery person smiled and left the room.

Barbie asked, "So who are they from? Open the card."

Everyone else in the verifications department also wanted to know. I had no clue.

I opened the card and read it aloud. "Thank you so much for the lovely conversation we had last night. I hope we can do it again. Please call me when you have some free time to talk." He had written his phone number on the card.

"Oooooohhhhh, Chery has an admirer." I was being taunted by some of the men.

"Oh come on, really? I don't think that it's anything serious at all. We just had a nice conversation; that's all," I said, trying to defend myself, not really sure I knew where this whole thing was really going.

There were a few phone calls made in the days to come. I started to wonder more about this situation and had someone look into it further for me. I found out he was married and having problems at home. I quickly ended the whole thing. I didn't want anything to do with a mess like that.

Not too long after that whole ordeal happened, I had another big blow to deal with. I had known for a while, that MCI wasn't supposed to hire relatives for the same department. When the accident happened, the company found out that Dawn and I were sisters. After they found out that I was okay and that the insurance had paid for all the bills, they gave Dawn and me an ultimatum. One of us was going to have to quit. They couldn't have us working in the same department. We weren't even in the same one anymore; but it didn't matter. We also were two of the best sales representatives for the company. That didn't matter either. Since Dawn was still trying to get back into school and I wasn't, I had decided that I would quit and return home to Alaska.

I spent the next few weeks trying to get all my stuff either sold or sent home by my mom's friends, who were driving up the Alcan (Alaska/Canada) Highway to Alaska in a big truck.

There were a few days where I also needed rides to get to work until my last day, which was the end of May. I was lucky enough to get some help from Jason's sister, Chris. She was always more than happy to get me where I needed to go. She still wasn't doing too well, with her cancer coming back and had been going through some radiation and chemotherapy treatments. I was really starting to get worried about her. The next thing to do was a bone marrow transplant. Finding a donor would be a hard thing to do. I continued to pray for her. I was told the best option is usually a relative.

In May, I decided to have a party for all the people who helped me in the accident. I wanted to show how appreciative I was to everyone who helped me through all this. I not only invited friends and family, but my doctors, attorney, and even

Thank you cake for party

the pilots who flew over and found me. I tracked them down through the hospital and was able to invite them. They were the last ones I ever expected to show up.

The day came for the party and my mom had even flown back for a visit and was able to attend. We set up the commons area in the front of the complex and had music, played pool, as well as foosball, and had lots of food and goodies to munch on. I had gone across the street to Subway and purchased a six-foot long sub for everyone. That was fun to try to cross the street with. About an hour into the party, the front doors opened and in walked two men in uniforms.

"Hi. Can I help you find someone?" I asked.

"We're looking for the party that we were invited to," one replied.

"Are you the two pilots from the helicopter? I really didn't think that you'd be able to make it," I said, surprised and pleased at the same time.

"Well, we're actually working, but we couldn't pass this up. No one has ever thanked us for helping them with the situations they've been in."

"You're kidding, right?"

They looked at each other and both replied, "No. We haven't even received a card to thank us for the help."

"I see that you're in uniform. Where's the helicopter?"

They again both looked at each other and replied with a smile, "We actually landed on the golf course just behind the complex and hopped the fence. We can't leave it there for too long, but they're closed right now." We all just laughed. I had to give them both a big hug.

"Well, come on in and help yourself to any of the food and drink you'd like," I said. I walked them over to the food and drinks counter. "I'm really glad you could make it."

My mother finally got a chance to sit and talk with them for a bit, while I had to mingle with some of the other guests. She expressed her deepest appreciation for everything they did for me, to keep me alive and for just being there. In the meantime, they just kept looking at me. They were actually staring. I finally noticed this and walked back over to them.

"I've noticed that you guys keep staring at me," I said.

"We just can't believe that you're the actual person we picked up that day. You were so beat-up from that truck. Your jaw was broken and one side of your mouth was touching the other side of your mouth. Now, WOW! Your doctors did a wonderful job of fixing you up. You can't even tell where they worked on you."

"Well, thank you. I want to thank you for all that you did. I know you guys just showed up, but man...what timing!"

"We weren't even supposed to be there. We were on our way to a call that was for another transport and decided to take a shortcut in the flight path. We shouldn't have even been there. When we were flying over, it looked like the accident had just happened. We called it in and it hadn't even been reported yet. If we hadn't been there, you never would have made it out of that trail. It's like we were supposed to be there. It's the only thing that makes any sense," he said.

"Well, I've got to have a picture taken with the both of you. You guys are my true heroes, you know!"

Me and the two pilots,
MY HEROS

Me and my two awesome dentists

I got between them both and put my arms around them and smiled, as big as I could. I still have this as my Facebook page picture today. They had to leave as soon as the picture was over and get back to the helicopter and work. I will never forget them. However, I don't know if I ever got their names. That's okay. I have their picture. It was a great party that went over very well. I was surprised, however, that my attorney never showed up. We should always thank any and all medical evacuation pilots. They help the needy in situations that would likely have a deadly outcome. They are a very rare breed and need our appreciation. You never know when you may be the one who's in need.

About a week before leaving MCI, I received my first settlement check from State Farm. It was the minimum I could get from my mom's insurance to help pay for bills and things. The second check would come later, after I arrived back in Alaska. The second check was the minimum that the driver's wife had placed on their vehicle. Had she not done this, the vehicle would have not been covered at all. Receiving the first check when I did really helped with getting back home and getting a restart on life. I also gave some money to my sister to get her back into school, after dropping out to be with me at the hospital. The total of the two checks were nowhere even near what the bills I had, totaled. My insurance through MCI, however, decided to cover everything for the hospital bills. When they found out that my settlement was so small, they thought I should keep it for future needs that may come up. I really appreciated them for doing that. I was very devoted to MCI. I wanted to work for them again, if they were ever to make it to Alaska.

Renee received three times as much as I did from the life policy that Jason and I had agreed to.

I had learned that my younger sister, Wendy, went to work for my dad in Ocala, Florida, that summer, and was still there. I set up a trip to go see her and my dad, whom I hadn't seen since I was ten years old. I made this trip in the middle of June. It about killed me. I went from

100-degree weather with almost no humidity in Phoenix, to 95-degree weather and 95 percent humidity. I got so sick while I was there.

We went to lots of places and saw a great many things. Sea World and Fort Lauderdale were the two most fun things we did. I didn't make it to Disney World. It was too far to drive, as my dad was still working while I was visiting. I did start to feel better after leaving on the airplane though.

CHAPTER 13

A Trip I Will Never Forget

Before I left to go back to Alaska, Sam and Cindy Meranto asked if Renee and I would like to join them in a trip to Beverly Hills for an awards ceremony. The Golden Boot Awards, which I had never heard of, was a ceremony for the Western stars of television and movies. I was so excited! Of course, I was going to go! Sam explained how expensive this could be and I didn't care. The money Renee and I had just received would more than pay for a quick trip there. This would happen at the end of June, the weekend before my trip home. We drove from Phoenix to Beverly Hills and it took about six hours.

When we arrived, all four of us checked into our hotel rooms. Renee and I had an awesome room with two huge beds and a window that looked out across the downtown area and the front of the hotel. You could see when people were arriving and what they were arriving in. I liked just watching all the Limos, Ferraris, and Porsches coming and going. Our bathroom was a separate room attached to the bedroom, but just as big. We were going to have so much fun. I just knew it.

I still needed to get a few things before the ceremony. Renee and I went downstairs to go through the lobby and see what we could find. They didn't have what we needed, so we went out and walked around the mall area on the other side of the street.

I was so amazed at how we were treated. I guess we weren't dressed properly or we didn't look like we should be there. The store employees would stand outside their shops and not let you in, if they didn't think you had the money to buy their items. I was a little offended. They had no idea that we had the money on us, in cash even, and were ready to buy exactly what we needed, if they would just help us. I finally found a place that had what I needed and purchased my last items for the evening. Walking back to the hotel, the same employees were still standing outside their stores. I just showed them that I had gotten what I needed from the store that would let me buy from them. I told them to never judge a book by its cover, because money wasn't the issue; they were. Keep in mind, this was June of 1990, and *Pretty Woman* had just been released in March. I had to laugh when I saw the same thing happen to me that happened to Julia Roberts in the movie. We walked back to the hotel to start getting ready for the events of the evening.

Renee and I had dressed in Western wear that was very fitting for the event. I had a jean skirt with a snakeskin belt, shin high-heeled boots, a jean shirt with frills on the front, a Western style watch, and earrings that looked like jean material. I had gotten my nails painted and went to a hair salon before we left Phoenix. After Renee finished getting ready, we headed down to the lobby. While she was still doing her last touch-ups, I looked out our window and it was about sunset with just enough light to use headlights, but we were still able to see well. I watched Limo after Limo pull up to the hotel, as people would get out in very elegant gowns and tuxedos. This was it! It's what I was hoping for; it was a long time coming. I just wasn't sure if I would recognize anyone. I hadn't really followed Westerns up to this point in my life.

We met Sam and Cindy in the lobby area. They wanted us to walk in with them, as they were invited and we were their guests. The evening was to include dinner during the award ceremony as well. We had one table all to ourselves, which was great. We entered the main hall to find our table and then went back out to the front commons area to mingle with the celebrities as they arrived. This was the first time they had allowed the public to mix and mingle with the celebrities. The Western stars were not getting as much attention as they used to, with all the new movies coming out. This event was hopefully going to boost the movie business back into making more Westerns again.

Renee and I hung out with our cameras to get as many pictures as we could of the stars. Sam and Cindy went off to talk with the stars that they knew personally. That night, we met and got pictures with Burt Reynolds, Steve James, Emilio Estevez, Bruce Boxleitner, and many, many more.

When I got to meet Steve James, who was from the movie *American Ninja*, we sat and talked for probably an hour about his film career,

Above: Bruce Boxlightner and me
Right: Steve James and me

karate in his movies, and my ambitions of being a screenwriter. He gave me so many tips and asked for my address so he could send me more information. He was one of the last people I would ever think to help me out with my dream, but he did. He motivated me to get my writing degree and wrote me a letter encouraging me to pursue my dreams and never to let them die. I also received a signed photo of him. I tried later to find him on Facebook once it came out. He has since passed away, but he will never be forgotten in my mind.

I kept seeing Emilio Estevez walking around and photographers getting pictures with him. He was with a woman who I'd never seen before. I knew he was having problems with Paula Abdul, but I wasn't sure who she was at the time. We couldn't get close to him initially.

While we were eating, we found his table. It was on the main floor, right below us. We weren't allowed to take any pictures in the gallery during the awards ceremony. We did, however, want to get pictures with him before he left and we didn't know how long he'd be there. After we finished eating, both of us decided we were going to see if he'd take a picture with us. We got up from our table and slowly walked over to the stairs and saw him. As we approached the table, we knelt down and tapped him on the shoulder.

"Excuse me, Emilio. Would you mind taking a picture with us?" Renee asked.

"Sure," he said politely. He put his arm around Renee. I backed up just a bit and snapped a picture with a flash. It caught the eye of one of the security and they approached us.

"Excuse me folks, but there's no pictures allowed during the ceremony.

Emilio Estevez and me

You can't do that here." He made sure we heard him and then he turned his back and left.

"Oh well," I said. "Maybe afterward." I shrugged my shoulders and was going to head back up to the stairs, after handing Renee her camera.

Emilio looked around and then back at us and said, "Hey, come here. If we do this quickly, they won't even know. C'mon, let's do this." He just smiled at me. I went over to his side and he put his arm around me and had a slight smile on his face. Renee took the picture. We said thanks and ran off as fast as we could. We went back to the table, expecting someone to come over and ask us to leave. No one ever did. Whew!

After the ceremony was over, everyone went back out into the commons area. We got some more pictures with Emilio before he left. He was a very good sport about it all. It was really awesome to meet people who I had only seen on TV or in movies. I wanted to do this every year, if Sam and Cindy would let me, but I also knew that this was probably a once in a lifetime event. It didn't matter; I had been there and that's all that mattered to me and I had the pictures to prove it.

The trip home was very quiet and satisfying, knowing what I had just accomplished. I was so excited about getting the pictures developed. I didn't have time to do it before I left to go back home. I'd have to wait. The next leg of my adventure was about to begin, not too long after arriving back in Phoenix.

CHAPTER 14

The Phone Calls Back Home

I finished out my time in Phoenix and went back home to Alaska. I was glad that I had a little money so I could sit back and relax for a bit, before really having to get back into the workforce again. I initially spent some time with friends who had a room for me, until I was able to find a place of my own.

I eventually found a very nice townhouse type apartment that I would move into. I got all my furniture and items that I shipped back up and moved into my new place, with help from some old friends. Since I didn't have any bedroom furniture, I knew this was an opportunity to buy brand-new ones instead of used. I went into Town and Country and bought a bedroom set, dining room set, and living room accessories to match my other furniture. I was pleased with how my placed looked.

I still didn't have a car yet, so I bought a brand-new 1990 Honda CRX, stick shift, black with red pin stripes and directional wheels. It was completely decked out with a sunroof, automatic door-locks, alarm system, AM/FM radio, and CD player. I thought this was awesome, to have a brand new car with all the gadgets. However, I didn't have a driver's license yet to actually be able to drive it. I knew I was going to have to be able to get around on my own, without the help of anyone else. Bruce, my friend from high school, taught me how to drive in the fall of that year.

I don't remember how long I had been in the apartment, when I received the phone call from Arizona. I do remember it was a very sunny, blue sky, and warm day. I had been cleaning my place all day long. I had been thinking about Jason and Arizona a lot, wondering how everyone was doing these days. I had been pondering about how the criminal court case was moving forward in Phoenix, with the truck driver. I was waiting for a call from my attorney, to let me know when the court dates were so I could buy a plane ticket to show up for the trial.

When the phone rang, I wasn't expecting this.

"Hello."

"Hello, is this Chery Schultz?" the voice asked.

"Yes, may I ask who's calling?" I didn't recognize the voice on the other end of the line and was curious to know who was calling me.

"Yes, you don't know me, but I'm one of the people who was at your accident scene in Arizona." His voice sounded excited and relieved, at the same time. "I've been trying to track you down for a while now. I finally was able to reach the Robbe family and they gave me your number, in Alaska. I hope that was okay." He was cautious to give out the last bit of information, not knowing my reaction.

"Uh, yeah, that's...okay. How did you...?" I didn't get to finish my question before he stopped me.

"I'm so glad that I finally found you. I know this is kind of a crazy call and you don't even know who I am, but your accident made such an impression and changed so many lives after what was experienced, at that scene." I was silent, not even knowing what to say. "Are you sitting down?" he asked.

"No, why?"

"You might want to, after what I've got to tell you."

I went ahead and pulled over a chair from the dining room table and said, "Okay, I'm sitting now." My heart was racing. I didn't know what to think or even say.

"My name is Dan Story. I don't know if you're a religious person or not, but the group I was with are all part of a fellowship that gets together and spends time away from it all. The real world, I mean. We're all in the spotlight most of the week with our jobs and need an outlet. We had all decided to go hiking, on that day. A few of us work as EMTs, some in the news and others at the TV station. Do you have a religious background at all?"

"Yes, I'm a Christian since I was a little girl," I answered. "Why?" I was wondering where this conversation was heading.

"First, I want to ask how you are doing. We never got to hear how things went after you left by helicopter that day. We briefly saw the accident, reported on the news and in the paper, but then we all lost track of you and just wondered if you were even alive. It took a while for me to track you down, with no information to go off of."

"I'm fine. Life has been a hard road for a while, but I'm back home and feeling like I'm finally going to be able to get things back on track again. Well, after the trial actually gets taken care of anyway. I'm still waiting to hear from my attorney, so I can fly back when the case goes to court," I told him.

"Well, when we heard the accident happen, we weren't too far from you at all. We rushed over to you guys and Joe. He was sitting on top of the guy who hit you, beating and holding him down the best he could, by himself. A couple of guys went over to help him secure the guy. Three of us went to Jason first and found him to be dead on impact. We heard you coughing and gasping. The two EMTs went over to you and tried to keep you alive the best they could. Knowing how far out we were, with no way of getting help soon, we sent one of the guys who was helping Joe, to drive into town as fast as he could, to get help. The rest of us stayed behind to help you." He paused, waiting to see if I was still with him in this conversation. "Are you doing okay?"

"Yes, I'm fine. Keep going," I said, waiting intently for what I may be hearing next.

"As we were trying to determine what to do with the both of you, there all of a sudden was this...presence. I don't know how else to describe it. When I first felt it, I looked up and around at everyone else in the circle around Jason. We were all looking at each other with blank stares on our faces. I asked everyone if they felt something. Everyone just nodded yes and couldn't even speak. It was hard to determine if it was the spirit of Jason waiting, hovering over his body to wait and see if you were going to make it or not. Or, if it was an angel ready and waiting to take Jason home, but we all knew it was something very spiritual," he said, still in awe, remembering how it all felt that day. "As soon as we saw the helicopter start to land and you were still breathing, coughing, and gasping, the presence was gone, as if it knew you were going to be okay and left the area. Again, I asked if everyone felt that same sensation. Again, they all agreed." He just stopped.

"I don't even know what to say. Are you telling me that either Jason, an angel, or possibly even God was there at the scene of the accident, waiting for me that day?" I asked hesitantly.

"Yes," he said. "I knew it was going to be a while before I could talk to you about this, with your injuries and all. Then, you left the state and I had to find out where you went. I had the most overpowering urge to find you and tell you what happened out there that day. You needed to know. Every one of us in the group that day has never forgotten the presence that was with us, and we never will," he said.

We had a great conversation. It must have lasted about two hours. After the call ended, I had to call my mom and let her know what just happened. It was another one of those amazing things that you never hear about.

About two to three weeks later, I received another phone call. It again was not the kind of information I was ready for, from my attorney this time. I was in the living room when the phone rang.

"Hello."

"Hello, is this Chery?" he asked.

"Yes it is and I know who this is. How's the case going?"

"Well, I have some information for you that you may not like. You might want to take a seat while I go through it with you," he said, as my heart jumped up into my throat and my stomach felt like it was twisting and flopping over and over. I wasn't ready for news that I didn't want to hear. I wanted news that I was ready to hear. I sat down in the dining room chair.

"Okay, go ahead. I'm ready."

"Up till now, the person who hit you has been pleading not guilty to the charges of manslaughter and first degree aggravated assault. We've been preparing for a trial to go to court and have a jury go through all of this, with us. That way we can get them to join in on what you've had to go through, this whole time and what you and Jason's family have lost out on. In the meantime, he has been talking to a lot of different attorneys trying to find someone who would defend him. It has come to my attention that he has found an attorney that is willing to represent him, as long as he pleads out with being guilty."

"Oh good, someone who's in their right mind to get him to actually face the fact," I said, hoping that now we could take care of this quickly.

"Now don't get too excited about this. It's not what you think it means."

I was a little concerned by this and didn't fully understand what he meant. "I don't understand. If he pleads out as guilty, we should be able to get him on manslaughter and aggravated assault, for the entire accountability of the accident, right?" I asked.

He said, "Well what this means is, if he pleads out as guilty, he then gets to ask for a barter arrangement. That means, he can ask for a shorter amount of time behind bars and a reduced sentence. Now, that's exactly what he's done. It would save the court system time and money and that's what they're all about these days."

As I was listening to him, my blood began to boil and my heart began to race. I wanted to go off on someone so bad, over this. "Okay, so if he accepts the blame, admits he was at fault for hitting us, and that he was drunk as well as being stoned, at the time, he will actually get less time, than if he was to come and to plea not guilty. Am I understanding this right?" I asked, confused and steadily increasing in anger.

"Yes, that would be correct. I'm sorry, but that's part of how the court system works," he said, in a very solemn voice.

"Then the court system SUCKS!" I said very loudly and angrily. "I think this guy should have to answer for everything he did! Not be able to just 'get off,' due to some court-preferred rule! I don't think that's fair at all!" I continued on my rampage of anger. "So if he gets a lighter sentence, what does that mean? Do you know what that sentence is, if I agree?" I asked, thinking that I had some sort of control over what would happen in this.

"Chery, you must understand. It doesn't matter if you agree or not. It's what the lawyers determine to be a fitting sentence for this case."

"So, do you agree with this nonsense of a bargain? I'm sure you don't if you're representing me, right?" I said, thinking again that I had some sort of control of this.

"Do I agree with this?" He took a long pause before answering. "Before I answer that, let me tell you what the outcome of this was. He'll get one year in prison then he'll have to have five years of what they call in-house probation. What that means is, he'll wear an ankle monitor and have to answer to his probation officer about where he goes and when, and how long he'd be gone. He can't go into bars or any place that has alcohol in it. The ankle monitor will go off if he goes outside his determined range for his house. He can go to and from work only, during the week. He'll be watched during the time frame when he's off work, how long the drive is to and from his house, and he has to call his probation officer when he gets home. He'll be serving his time, but at his house and not behind bars," he explained.

"I don't think I like the sound of this and where it's going. You do agree with this, don't you?" I said smugly.

"Yes, I agree with this. It's getting too full in the prison setting these days and the system is trying to find better ways of getting people the help they need, while still serving their sentences. This way, he'll be able to attend AA meetings as well as being watched over and accounted for. That doesn't mean that I agree with what he did, because I don't. I understand how this makes you feel, but in the eyes of the court system, this is fair justice."

"What you're telling me is...let me make sure I understand this correctly. He can get drunk and stoned, get behind the wheel of a vehicle, which is breaking the law already. Go crazy on back roads, that aren't supposed to even have cars or trucks on them, only off-road motorized vehicles. Hit and kill one person, send the other one into a coma for a long road to recovery and heartache, and this is somehow not deemed as someone who needs to be sent to prison? Shouldn't he be sentenced to the death penalty or something, for taking a life and causing lifelong injuries to another? Didn't you even tell me that he has a history of drinking and driving? I thought that if you had been caught more than two times they did some severe punishment. This guy, however, gets to go home and spend his life with his family, after one year of jail time! I, however, don't get to spend any more time with the person who he killed. I have to try to make sense of all this and fight to remember things in my past that I may never get back. So not only did he take my future away, but somehow he gets to take part of my past as well." I was ranting and raving all through my apartment over this information. "What's the reason for him being able to go home when others have to spend their entire time behind bars?" I asked.

"The reason I was given is, he's the sole provider for his family and without him his wife and kids wouldn't have any way of making it in the world. I checked on what he has for assets, to see if there was something else we could go after for your settlement. This guy...he has nothing. Everything he owns is, either double-mortgaged, broken, or he owes money on it. It seems as though, if we take anything from them, you will owe a ton of money and have nothing out of this. The only reason there was any insurance on the vehicle that hit you was that the wife had placed liability on it not too long before the accident."

"What was the amount of coverage that I'm covered for?

"There was only $50,000 coverage for this accident that you will be able to claim the full amount for."

"You do realize that doesn't even cover my hospital bills. They were over $100,000 last I'd been told. What am I supposed to do? I know that MCI's insurance is paying all those bills, but what about future expenses?" I started to cry.

"Yes, I realize that. I'm going to check and see if your mom's insurance will cover anything else, since you were in school and in Arizona for that. We will see what happens there," he replied.

"So what am I supposed to do now? Am I still coming down there for a hearing or something?" I asked, sniffing and drying my eyes.

"No, you're not needed at this point. The judge will be ruling on the arrangement in the next couple of weeks. What my recommendation to you is, write a letter to the judge, explaining how you feel about the plea and what you think should happen to him. Maybe, this could change the sentence to a better-fitting one, for you. That is rare, but you never know. For now, you'll just have to wait and see what the judge rules for the final sentence on this. I'll call you and let you know when this happens."

"I don't even know how to feel right now. Except, I feel violated and robbed. I guess I don't have any choice in the matter since I'm up here in Alaska. Does the Robbe family know about this yet?" I asked.

"I believe that their attorney was calling them today as well. I'll be in touch and again, I'm so sorry for everything that you've had to go through."

"I'll be waiting and where do I send the letter to the judge?"

"Just mail it to my address and I'll get it to him," he said.

"I'll do that. Thank you for the information. Goodbye." I hung up the phone.

I used the anger I had, to write a letter to the judge. In it, I said how if Arizona had a death penalty, I would like to be the one to throw the switch. In the end though, it's not going to be any of us that makes the final judgment on this. As I was writing the letter, I felt something come over me and learned that nothing will change to bring Jason back. The final judgment comes from God and that will be the toughest sentence to have to deal with. I told the judge that whatever the sentence is, I would eventually have to accept it and move on with my life, even if I didn't agree with what it was. I still think that the sentence should have been much harsher than it was.

I found out later that the in-house probation, at that time, was a joke. They didn't even have enough people to maintain all the ones they had placed on in-house probation. They were coming and going as they pleased, most of the time. I also realized, by doing what they did with him, he could still drink at home, just by having his wife go buy alcohol for him and he doesn't even have to leave the house. So what's the point in that? I always wondered how much of a lesson he actually learned. I might as well play the game of Russian roulette, to see if everything goes as planned or not. It seemed his odds were way better than mine.

I spent a lot of time crying again after that.

CHAPTER 15

Jobs

I tried to stay as busy as I could, but wasn't ready to go back to work just yet. I was still trying to challenge my brain to remember people's names that I should have known or recently met, even earlier that day. It wasn't easy. I still ran into times where I couldn't complete a sentence and remember what I was talking about or where I was going with the thought I had. To this day, I still have a hard time matching names to faces. It's hard to know that you know someone and can't think of their name, even when you've known them for years.

It came to the first-year anniversary of the accident. I had gotten the opportunity to go to Hawaii and to use my sister's friend's timeshare. I invited Renee and another friend, Lauren, to go with me to spend a week there. We had a blast! We spent a lot of time at Waikiki Beach and went to the zoo, as well as the International Market Place for shopping. I met some very interesting people there. At the end of the trip, I didn't

Me at Planet Hollywood in Hawaii

want to go home. It was about that time, I knew I would have to start looking for work.

After being home for about a week, Renee was calling me to let me know that Chris hadn't been doing well and was back in the hospital full time. I told her to keep me informed and that I'd be praying for her and the family. I wasn't looking for work too hard yet, just because I wasn't sure if I was going to need to fly back to Arizona again soon. I spent time looking around for what was available and the types of jobs out there that I might be able to perform without too many problems.

Renee had done a bone marrow transplant with Chris. It was supposed to be the perfect match and probably the best bet to correct the problem. But Chris's body wouldn't accept the bone marrow and started to reject Renee's transplant. At that time, things started to really go downhill fast for her.

I think it was the first or second week in December when I got the phone call from Renee. I was at the house of a guy that I'd been dating. My mom was at my place and called me on the phone late that night, telling me that Chris had passed away in the hospital. As soon as I got off the phone with her, I jumped on getting a plane ticket back down to Arizona as soon as possible. I was there the next day. The Robbes met me at the airport when I arrived. It was so hard to believe, but we knew the day was coming.

I couldn't believe what this family has been through in just one year alone. They went from a family of five, to a family of three in just about a year. Renee was dating Bobby, who was Joe's younger brother and that seemed to be a good thing for her.

Chris had been the one to receive Jason's car after he passed away, and now it would go to Renee. It was great to see the Prelude still being kept in the family and taken care of. I sat in it a few times, just for old times' sake. We had Chris's funeral a few days after I was there and it was hard. I at least got to say goodbye to her, one more time. It was the first funeral I had ever been to and they had an open casket. Chris looked fake and waxy almost. She was cold and stiff when I touched her for the last time. I said that I would never do another open casket again. It was the last time I saw her and that's what stuck in my head from then on. I would like to have been able to think about her as I had remembered her. I still do, but it's not the same when the last time keeps showing back up. I guess it may have been a blessing that I wasn't able to go to Jason's funeral. I only have memories of him alive and well and very energetic to be around. I did get lots of pictures from Jason's funeral from his dad and got to see what he looked like in the casket, but it wasn't the same as being in person. Jason just looked like he was sleeping in those pictures. My sister Dawn also told me that when she went to his funeral, that's how he looked to her as well. You couldn't tell how bad the injuries were on him, because it had been his chest that was crushed.

Just before I left Alaska to go to Phoenix, I had called Renee to give her my itinerary for the trip. We had a nice talk and she gave me some insight as to what happened, right before Chris passed away.

Just before Chris had passed away, she was in a deep sleep. In her room, she had her mom, dad, Renee, and her fiancé, Raymond. Renee said they could hear Chris mumbling in her sleep and having some sort of a conversation in her dream, but they couldn't figure out what was being said. This went on for a long while, until Chris finally woke up to everyone surrounding her asking, how she was doing. They asked her about the dream she'd been having and said it must have been a good one. Chris proceeded to tell them that she'd been talking with Jason. Everyone was startled. She said she'd been talking with him about many different things and that she was needed on the other side to help him with something. He reassured her that everyone here was going to be fine and that she could go ahead and let go of her body to follow him, in her new journey. She was very calm and peaceful about it all. She got to say goodbye to her family and fiancé, closed her eyes, and then passed away. Not many people get that kind of an exit. She will be forever remembered. I spent about a week with her family and then returned to my home in Alaska.

When I got home, I set up my place for Christmas. I had to buy all kinds of brand-new items. My place looked very cheery that year. I spent a lot of time with my family and close friends. I didn't want to miss out on anything with not knowing when or where my time may come up. I got through Christmas and my funds from the accident were starting to deplete after investments and purchases made. I had purchased triple-A bonds and a brand-new car. Like I said earlier, I also furnished my apartment.

After the New Year, I got a job in the town mall at a store called Discovery Imports. I worked there for a few months until I heard that the local phone company was expanding and wanted to hire some telemarketers, to get the word out in the state. I applied for a job with them as a residential telemarketer, again. I knew the job pretty well, working for the country's second largest company for a year and a half. I got the job and quit my other one. I helped out as much as I could and trained people with the knowledge I was able to bring over. I was able to advance to commercial telemarketing for about one month. The company had used all their marketing money on TV advertising to compete with the number one company and as a result they ran out of money to pay us. One week before Christmas, they fired us all. I was heartbroken. I spent all the money I had on presents and had nothing to give the guy I was dating at the time.

We got through that. Then I went to work for a State Farm office as a receptionist. I really liked the job, until I was asked to do a couple of things that only a sales representative was supposed to do. I decided to leave that job, so I wouldn't get into any sort of trouble. After that, I saw an ad in the newspaper for a receptionist at the local credit union and went to work there.

In the meantime, I had gotten married in June of 1991 to the guy I had been dating since January of that same year. Let's just call him Stu. We had a trailer on about one acre of land and two dogs. His parents owned a thriving business in Wasilla. Things were looking up. After working at the credit union for about a year, I wasn't feeling like I was going to be able to make much more money and started to look for a new job. We hadn't talked about kids too much, and I wasn't planning on having any for a while. I had my reasons for this. My family and some of my friends didn't like the way I was treated by him.

On my lunch breaks at work, I had started looking through the help-wanted ads in the newspapers. I kept seeing the same one over and over and over. It was for a chiropractic assistant in a busy Wasilla clinic. I kept putting it off because I figured you'd have to have some sort of training for that kind of job. I couldn't find anything else in the paper that was a secure job.

One day at church, our new pastor was giving his first sermon. I had been listening to his every word and then getting another message on top of his, also being heard very loud and clear. It had to do with finding a new job. I was so frustrated and confused about the job that I started to cry at the end of the sermon. I excused myself and went to the bathroom. I had been praying a lot about what job to take and what I could do. I went into a stall and closed the door, locking it behind me. No one else was in the bathroom. I prayed out loud, but softly so no one outside could hear me.

"Lord, I heard you talking to me in the sermon. I know you have something you want me to do, but I don't know what it is. I will listen, if you can just give me a sign or show me where you want me to go," I said.

After I finished praying the door opened to the bathroom and an elderly woman with a walker came in. I think she had a bad back. As soon as I saw her, I knew what I was supposed to do.

I quit crying, wiped my tears, and said, "Okay, I understand. I know now; I need to apply for that job that keeps popping up in front of me. I'll call tomorrow."

I went back out to the congregation and fit myself back into my spot, with a smile.

I was asked if everything was okay and I said, "It is now."

The next day, I went to work and on my lunch break made that call about the job, thinking that it would probably be gone by now. I had an interview set up later that week, after my work hours. It was about the beginning of December in 1993. I made it over to the interview and felt pretty good about it. They had me wait out in front, and told me before I left, that I had gotten the job. I started within about one to two weeks after that.

If what happened at church had not happened, I never would have tried for that job. I believe I was told over and over about the job and didn't listen until I had a direct answer to a question that I'd asked. This happens more than anyone knows. It's just opening up and listening to what you're being told and not doubting the result.

I worked at this job for a little over five years before leaving it. I had gotten a divorce from my first husband in 1996 due to things that weren't acceptable to me and threats he had made.

During the time with my husband, I was at home a lot by myself and was able to take a writing course through the mail. It was with The Institute of Children's Literature in West Redding, Connecticut. It took a couple years to do it, but I was glad when I finished and had a degree in writing. My instructor and I got along great. I had told him that I wanted to write movie scripts and he told me his son went to Hollywood to become an actor.

One of my assignments was to create a story about a natural disaster and it was just supposed to be the beginning of it. I wrote one called "Tornado's a Comin'." I got an A for that paper. About six months later, he wrote to tell me that his son had gotten a role in the movie *Twister*. I was so happy for him. When the movie came out, I went to see it. It was really good. Months later, I was reading through my work again and found that the beginning of *Twister* had been just like my story for the assignment. I started to wonder about that and how much of a coincidence it was. It didn't matter, I was just happy that if it was my idea, I had enough creativity to get it into a movie.

The other thing I did, during this period of my life, was to prove to everyone in my ex-husband Stu's family that I could make things happen, if I put my mind to it. What I mean is, in Valdez, Alaska, they had been filming a movie there called *On Frozen Ground*. I wanted so badly to go there, just to watch them film. A few people had said that I'd just be wasting my time and that I'd never get close enough to anyone to even be able to watch what they were doing.

I said, "Watch me."

I took my mom and we went to Valdez for a weekend. We left early in the morning on Saturday, about six, and it took about four and a half to five hours to get there. We arrived and checked into the hotel. We went down to the pier where Mom wanted to check out the location of a boat that went into the inlet for a church session that was scheduled on Sundays. While we were there, we spoke to someone who knew what had been going on with the movie and told me where the headquarters were, if I wanted to talk with someone there. We went over to that location and I walked inside to find no one available. There were postings on the wall, telling of different locations for shots to be filmed. As I was standing there, flipping through papers, someone came out of the back room.

"Hi. Who are you?" he asked.

"Anyone you want me to be," I replied, not even thinking about what I was saying and to whom I was saying it to. I smiled and turned to him, not even getting his name.

"My name is Chery. I just drove in from Wasilla to see what you guys are doing here. I was hoping to be able to get a glimpse of some filming. Do you know where the next shoot might be?" I asked, hoping he'd be willing to give me some kind of information.

"Are you on a roster or anything for a specific shoot?"

"No, I'm just very interested in filmmaking," I replied.

"Sorry, I can't give out any information to anyone not in the movie," he replied as he started to turn away.

"I thought that might be the case, but I just had to ask," I said sounding very disappointed. "Thanks anyway." I started to leave.

He stopped midway in his turning away and said, "Hey, if you want to try to see some of them or get pictures, there's a city thank you party going on tonight at the high school. You may be able to stand outside and get pictures at least. You could always ask the security guards there." He smiled, handed me a piece of paper, and continued walking down the hallway in front of him.

I was even more excited now than before. I had a location and time of where they were going to be. I went back out to the car with my mom, who had been standing there with me the whole time, shaking her head at how I just blended in.

"Anyone you want me to be? Really? Who says that kind of thing?" she asked, trying to figure out how and why I would say that to someone I didn't even know.

"I don't know; it just felt right to say it, and it obviously didn't hurt anything, did it?" We walked to the car. "It got me the information I needed to see everyone or maybe even talk to someone tonight."

"I don't know anyone who could have done, what you just did," she said, smiling.

"So what do we do till then?" I asked.

"Eat."

We went and got dinner, hung out at the hotel for a while, and relaxed until about six thirty. I drove us over to the school and parked the car in the normal school parking area and took only my camera with me and got out of the car.

"Aren't you coming with me?" I asked, as I saw my mom stay in the car.

"No, I think I'll stay here. You seem to do pretty well on your own and I don't want to get in the way of any progress you might make. I can see pretty well from here what's going on. Just leave me the keys, in case it gets cold or I want to listen to the radio," she said.

"Okay." I gave her the keys and headed up the hill to the front entrance. There were about four guys standing out in front, checking for tickets to get in.

"Hello, my name is Chery. I was wondering if it would be okay to just stand out front and take pictures of people as they arrive."

"Yes, that's fine. Just don't get in anyone's way. Are you with the paper?" they asked, curiously.

"Nope, just a fan from Wasilla that drove out today and is heading back tomorrow morning." I smiled really big. "Thank you for allowing me to do this."

Amazed, one guy replied, "You drove all the way from Wasilla, just to be here for less than a day and are driving back again? Why? Why, would you do something like that? Isn't it like six hours or something?"

"Yes, five and a half hours to be exact. It's a very pretty drive. I was hoping that I could see some filming being done, but they wouldn't give me any information on that."

"Yes, you can stand over there all night, if you want. I don't think anyone is going to mind at all." He pointed to where he'd like me to stand. I went over to the spot and stayed there, watching and waiting.

As people started to arrive, I was taking pictures of people who I thought might be in the movie. Some were just residents, set in as extras. I even went to check on Mom once or twice to make sure she was doing okay.

In the two to three hours that I was there, I got to meet Michael Caine and his wife. I also got pictures with him. He was really nice. I also met the production manager for the entire shoot. He came out to talk with me about halfway through the event.

"Hi," he said as he walked up to me.

"Hi," I replied, and thought I was going to be asked to leave.

"How's everything going? I see you're just taking pictures out here."

"Yes, they're for my personal collection." I smiled. "Is everything okay? It sounds like a lot of fun in there." I could hear all the commotion

Above: Mike the Production
Manager &me
Right: Michael Cain and me

going on inside the gym. They had left open the front door to get air in the building.

"It's a little hot in there tonight. I wanted to get some fresh air." He took a deep breath. "You haven't seen Steven Segal yet so far, have you?"

"No, I haven't. He is supposed to show, right?"

"He was told he needed to be here, but he sometimes does his own thing. I really hope he shows; this was an awfully nice thing the city did for us shooting the scene here." He sounded frustrated. We had a nice conversation for about fifteen minutes while he waited with me outside. "Tell you what, why don't you come inside and get something to eat, warm up a little, and then we can wait to see if he shows."

I didn't know what to say at first. "I want to thank you for your hospitality, but this party is for you and the crew. I don't want to intrude on your time," I said, very sincerely.

He asked, "What's your name?"

"Chery, and yours?"

"It's Mike. Nice to meet you." We shook hands and smiled at each other. "Tell you what. You are now on Steven Segal patrol. When you look over there," he pointed to the hill across the street, with a driveway that just disappears into the trees, "if you see a car come down that hill, let the men behind you know; that should be Steve's car arriving. I'm going to head back inside so they don't think I died or something. If you want to see some filming, there is one shot left that has to be redone tomorrow morning. It's a reshoot of the oilrig blowing up. Someone got in the way last time and got hurt. We have to do this one more time. If you meet me at the location, which I'll give you directions to, in the morning, I'll get you in to show you around and you might even be able to watch the shot being taken."

"That would be awesome!" I said. "I'll be there, no matter what. Do I just ask for you, when I arrive?"

"Yes, everyone will be getting ready for the shoot, but the guard at the gate will come get me."

"Okay, and I'll let you know if Steven shows up as well. Thank you so much," I replied, very happily. Steven never showed up for the party that night. Everyone wondered where he'd gone. They found out later that he'd gone bear hunting.

The next morning, I drove out to the site where the filming was being done. Mom again, decided to wait in the car. I wasn't very long on this trip. I went to the gate and was asked to wait, while they got the production manager. After Mike saw me, he came over and brought me inside the filming area. He showed me everything they had, behind-the-scenes. I was so excited. They started to set up for the shoot and both main actors were in their motor homes. I was allowed to stay in the tent that had all the big wigs in it. That was cool! They brought Steven Segal out of his trailer and he had a lot of makeup on. They shot the oilrig blowing up, right in front of me. I was so impressed. After the shoot was done, I thanked everyone and followed Steven out to his motor home. I asked him if I could get a picture with him and he agreed. However, the person who took the pictures didn't know how to use the camera, even after I showed him. The pictures never took. I didn't find this out till later, when I went to develop them, and no pictures with him showed up. It was a great trip though. I went home and told my story of what I got to do and had the pictures to prove it. I was even invited to go to Washington to film a scene there, if I could make it. I knew that I had other responsibilities that would keep me from being able to do this, so I unwillingly turned it down. I was sure my boss wouldn't let me go and I knew my husband Stu wouldn't want me to do it. I was right about my spouse, but my boss thought that would have been a great opportunity. I should have just done it. Opportunities like that don't just show up every day.

I got divorced in the summer of 1996. I didn't want to do it, but I just couldn't see myself living as I was for the rest of my life. God had to have something better for me to do in this life. I don't think he wanted me to be ruled and threatened by someone else.

I had moved back into the townhouse where I used to live. I thought it was funny that the same place was available, right when I needed it. It was only five minutes from where I worked. The only problem was, it was going to be too expensive to live there by myself. I could do it for a while, but not forever. I think I only stayed there for about four or five months, before I had to make a change.

I eventually moved in with a friend, to try to cut costs for both of us, and later found out that was also a bad situation to be in. I was only there for about three months. I really needed to find a place I could afford, and be on my own for a while.

I found a place on Knik Road that was affordable and close to work. I would have to share a Laundromat with all the other people who lived in the area, but it was doable. I gathered a few friends and moved into my new place. I was pretty happy with what I had found. My place was on the second floor, so I didn't have to worry about too much noise when I was home.

I went on a ten-day cruise with the chiropractic clinic from February 27 to March 12 of 1997. It was a training seminar for chiropractic assistants. That was a new beginning for me, after what I had just been through with my recent ex-husband. I met and hung out with Neil, the entertainment director on the cruise. He gave me a new way of looking at men and life, a new interpretation and perspective I had not seen

Me in black dinner dress on cruise

before. I was very grateful to him. I never saw him again after the cruise, which was to be expected. I did get one letter from him and hoped that he'd visit me in Alaska, but that never happened.

CHAPTER 16

Starting Over

Aﬅer just returning from the most wonderful trip I've ever had so far, I had a new outlook on life. I still wanted certain things in life that were always just out of reach, but I was semi-okay with where I was.

It was about two and a half weeks later that the most wonderful thing happened to me, even though at the time, I wasn't aware of it.

One night, I had gone out with my mom and some family friends. We went to the Mat-Su Resort to go karaoke singing. After we were done there, I wasn't tired yet so I decided to go to Wasilla Bar, where my friend, Bruce, from high school, worked. I went there and sat down at the end of the bar and was listening to the band. Bruce gave me a complimentary pop and talked for just a few minutes about how the cruise went, before having to get back to other patrons. I started to look around the room, noticing the different type of crowd that was there, with a hard rock band playing that night. The music was loud and I saw a lot of leather, spiked hairdos, facial piercings, and lots of smoking. I didn't want to be there much longer, just enough to finish my drink or maybe if they had some decent music during the band's break.

The band took their break and started playing intermission music. As soon as they played the "Macarena", I was on the dance floor. After the song was over, I went and sat back down for a little bit, trying to decide if I wanted to stay or leave. I didn't really know any of the people, so what was the point?

As I was about halfway done with my drink, the bar owner and a man in his late twenties came over to where I was sitting. There was a stool on each side of me that was available. The owner sat on my right side, in front of a Mega Touch video game, and started to play. The other man sat on my left side and ordered a beer.

They started talking across me and I started to feel a little funny. I kept leaning backward every time they wanted to talk.

I had been in there a few times and the owner knew me by name. She also knew me through Bruce.

She asked me, "So Chery, what do you think of this band?"

"Honestly, it's not my type of music. It's too loud and you can't really dance to it. It's more like head-banging music, which isn't my style. Really, I mean look around at the type of crowd that's in here." We glanced around the room. "I don't see the normal crowd that hangs out here with the pop bands. It makes me a little nervous too."

"Yeah, I see what you're saying. I thought I'd give them a try and see what they would do. I'm not sure that I will book these guys again," she said, looking a little frustrated.

"I think if you stick to the guys you normally hire, you would pack this place out every night; you'll do just fine," I said, with enthusiasm.

"I wanted to ask you because I know how much you like to dance and I see you in here a lot. Let me introduce you to someone. Steve, this is Chery. Chery, this is Steve Manning. He's one of my new morning shift bartenders."

I turned to shake his hand. "Hello."

"Hello. I just came by to get my new schedule for this next workweek, on my way home from Anchorage. I don't usually go out dressed like this," he said, laughing at himself with the way he was dressed. He had on a pair of jean pants, 49ers sweatshirt, and a navy jacket with a lot of different port patches on it, showing locations around the world that he'd been to.

As the owner and Steve proceeded to have a conversation across me, I was just about to leave and offer the seat to him. Bruce had been coming over and checking on our drinks and asking how everything was going, almost like a big brother would do.

"So you come here a lot, do you?" Steve asked.

"Almost every weekend, at some point. I like to dance and this is about the only place in town with a big enough floor to get around on. The music is good, most of the time, and I like playing pool as well," I said.

"I just started working here, not too long ago. I was in the navy for the last nine years. I just got out in October and moved back up here. My dad has lived here ever since I got out of high school. He's the only family I've got, so I moved back here to be with him. How long have you been here?"

"I was born here on Elmendorf Air Force Base, but we moved around a lot with my dad being in the military. My parents divorced when I was ten, and we moved back here, where most of my mom's family had come to live, and I've been here ever since. I actually just came down here to talk with Bruce, who I went to high school with, and have a drink before heading home for the night. I was getting ready to leave, just as you both sat down." I took my glass of pop and finished it off.

"Well, don't leave just yet. We just started talking, he said with a smile, trying to get me to stay and talk a little longer.

Just as he said this, the band took a break and they were playing regular music again between sets. "The Electric Slide" started to play and I had to get up and dance.

"Oh, that's my song. Gotta go! Bruce can you watch my coat and things here and I'll be right back?" I asked, very excited as I placed my coat back onto the stool and headed toward the dance floor.

He said, "Yeah, it'll be fine."

I sprinted out to the middle of the floor and got in line. I love to dance to "The Electric Slide." After the song ended, I went back to my seat and was a little winded.

"Sorry for interrupting the conversation, but when that song plays, I have to be out there on the dance floor," I said, with a big smile. The ice cubes that had been in my glass, had melted and I drank the little bit of water in the bottom. Bruce saw this and brought me over another drink. "Well, thank you Bruce. What do I owe you?" He just waved his hand off not to worry about it. "Thank you again." I looked over at Steve; I guess I can't leave just yet, with a complimentary drink like that." I smiled and took a sip.

"You do like to dance, don't you?" Steve asked with a smile, hoping that I would continue to talk with him.

"I told you I did," I said. "It's my workout every weekend. I love to do it as much as I can. What about you? Do you dance?"

"Yes, yes I do."

"Hmm. I guess I'll have to see one night, when you're in here not working. Right now, I have to go. I've got to get some sleep. I have to wake up early." I started to put on my jacket and finished off my drink. "Thanks again, Bruce. Have a good night." I smiled and waved at him. He was busy and just turned and waved back at me.

"If you don't mind, can I walk you out to your car?" asked Steve.

"I don't mind. I think that would be fine."

I said good night to the bar owner and walked out the door. As we were walking over to where my car was, Steve carried on the conversation. "So what are you doing tomorrow? Can I call you?"

I stopped walking and turned to look at him. "I'm going to church in the morning. Then tomorrow night, I'm going to Anchorage to a theater production at Anchorage Baptist Temple. I'll be busy most of the day."

"What about on Monday?"

"I have very weird work hours and it's really hard to get time in the evenings to do anything. Most of my free time is on the weekends."

"What about lunch? You have to eat lunch, right?" he said, looking for anything that I would be willing to do.

"I can probably try to do lunch on Monday, but it's got to be close to the office. I'm on Main Street and Swanson, at the chiropractic clinic on the corner."

"How about going to Country Kitchen? It's close and I can pick you up," he replied, hoping to get a hook in this time.

"That sounds good. I haven't been there in a while. I'll probably have to meet you there though. I don't always get off right when I'm supposed to. Just be there about one-fifteen and I'll be as close to that as I can. How does that sound?"

"Great! I'll see you then. Have a good night and drive home carefully."

"I will, thank you." I got into my car and Steve started to walk back into the bar. Just as I was leaving the parking lot, I turned to look to my left and saw Steve doing a little happy dance with a small jump and arm pump, as he walked back up the stairs onto the deck. I just laughed.

Little did I know that the one night I was not expecting to find anyone, I found the one I would spend the rest of my life with!

CHAPTER 17

The Courtship

We went on our first lunch date and it was just fine. He asked me out for a second date and I eventually accepted. Steve was about 5 feet 10 inches and had short dark brown hair with brown eyes. His build looked like he should be a police officer or something. He was wide on the top with a small waist and strong legs. He used to swim in high school and was on the swim team. His last post in the navy was in Hawaii for three years with the Navy Seals. He worked out with them a lot doing physical training, so it did explain a lot.

I remember while we were dating, the hardest thing for Steve was Neil, the entertainment director from the cruise. I was looking forward to seeing him again and Steve wasn't thrilled in the slightest by this. Steve would be at my place, when he wasn't working, trying to spend as much time with me as he could. I just kept saying, "Let's just be friends and see what happens."

Guys, however, don't seem to like that a lot, but Steve didn't mind. He went through a lot trying to get my attention off Neil and onto him.

I never thought that anyone would ever put so much time into trying to make me happy.

Soon I was having a hard time not liking Steve. I remember telling one of the girls I worked with, that I was having a hard time not liking him and she just laughed.

After about two weeks of dating, I was housesitting for Bruce's mom. Steve had just dropped me off at the house. We were in the driveway; I was getting ready to get out of the car, and out of the blue he told me that someday he was going to marry me. I didn't know what to say at first, but I thought he had a lot of nerve coming right out and saying that, after just two weeks of dating. He also knew that I was still waiting to hear from Neil about visiting me in Alaska. I wasn't completely sold on being with anyone in particular at that point.

Steve was on a dart team and asked me to come watch him play. He then tried to convince me to play with him, in the summer dart league. I had never played darts before. I knew I wasn't going to be very good. I said, I'd think about it.

April rolled around and a dart team needed an extra player for Vegas; they drafted Steve for a trip to the International Dart Tournament. He didn't want to go and just leave me, but he couldn't let his team down either. He'd been with them longer than me. He went to Vegas and called me every chance he got. I thought that was a little odd. I know that if I were in Vegas, I'd be all over the place having fun, not sitting by the phone waiting to make a call. He told me later that he couldn't stop thinking about me. He came back early when his team got eliminated. When his teammates came back, I found out that he had been in his room most of the time, waiting to call me instead of having fun. It made me feel good that he was so dedicated to spending time with me.

During May and June, we spent a lot of time together. I realized that he might be the one I was always looking for. He loved being with me all the time. I never had to worry about what he was doing or thinking. He didn't make rude comments or call me names, which was nice for a change. We had a lot in common and could even finish each other's sentences. We were so similar that people thought we were brother and sister rather than a couple dating. I just enjoyed not fighting all the time. The time we spent together was very enjoyable.

In July, we were at my apartment playing backgammon. I went to use the bathroom and when I came back, it was my turn to roll the dice. When I did, a ring came rolling out of the cup. I stopped and looked up at Steve. He took the ring, got down on one knee, and asked me to marry him. I was very surprised and couldn't say a word initially. I, of course, said, "Yes." We agreed to get married on the one-year anniversary of when we met, March 29. I was excited and scared at the same time. I didn't want the same thing happening again that happened with my first marriage.

I called my sister Wendy in Pennsylvania. I told her what had just happened. She said, "Congratulations!" I also wished her a happy birthday, since it was her birthday in just two days. That makes it easy to remember what day it was. We talked for a bit longer and I went back to my game.

The one thing I did ask of Steve was to never be controlling of me, to tell me who I could or couldn't talk with, and where I could or couldn't go. I got him to promise that he would never do that to me. I counted on that and would never forget those words.

At that time, he was living with his dad and so I decided that with as much time as he was spending with me, he should just move into my apartment. Now, I knew that my mom and grandmother would both have a cow because of our religious beliefs. I told her I was not about to go through that same thing I did with the first marriage and that

I wanted everything out in the open from the very beginning. Mom wasn't too happy about the setup, but she did say that she understood. With her being on her third marriage, I knew she would.

Steve knew that I was still having problems with short-term memory and forgetting names of people I've known for years and it didn't matter to him. He would help me whenever he had the chance, to remember about anything and everything. It helped that he had a well of useless knowledge in his head. That's what he called it anyway. He could remember all kinds of tidbits from things that really didn't mean anything, but that came in handy when playing certain games.

We got married March 29, 1998, at the Best Western in Wasilla. It was a great turnout and even my dad came to the wedding. Steve's mom also showed up. That would be the last time either of us would ever see either of those parents again. They chose to not be a part of our lives and it was frustrating for both of us, but we learned to accept it and go on.

That night, we stayed in one of their suites and had a steak and prawns dinner with a bottle of champagne. It was the happiest I'd ever been at that point in my life. We went to Vegas on one of our paid dart tournaments, for our honeymoon. That was a fun trip. For my wedding present to him, I bought Steve an autographed full-size Joe Montana helmet because he's such a 49er fan.

Things went well for a long time. We never really had a fight, just agreed to disagree about a few things and moved on. We bought some property and had a house built on it. We had even purchased a timeshare in Vegas to go to when we weren't playing darts. After I started playing darts with Steve, we eventually became the team to beat. We would win a trip to Vegas every winter and when the summer league was going, we won a trip on that one too. The great part about those trips was that the league paid for everything except your food and entertainment. It was a vacation twice a year.

I quit working at the chiropractic clinic in March of 1999. We had been talking about having a family and I needed better insurance than what I had. Steve knew the regional manager for Fred Meyer Jewelers, and we had talked with him a few times. It was also how I got such a beautiful wedding ring. Fred Meyer was opening a store in Wasilla soon, and they were hiring. I applied for the jewelry department, after the regional manager had told me how good a manager or assistant manager position would be. I got the job and trained in Anchorage for about six months, before the store opened.

I had my first son, Alexander Keith, in January of 2001. I had my second son, Clark Kent, in 2003. There is a story to their names as well, but I'll talk about that later. I was working at Fred Meyer both times, but left halfway through my second pregnancy. The first one was too hard on me, working six days a week twelve-hour days for Christmas, and they wouldn't let me wear comfortable maternity clothes. I had to wear heels and dresses on concrete floors. I just couldn't do it again. I also wasn't happy that the job I had been trained for, assistant manager, was given to someone else who hadn't been with the company as long as I had, and I had to teach her how to do her job. The reason I was given was that I was looking to start a family and they needed someone who could travel and not have to be home with their family. I found out much later, that she and the manager had been having an affair that ruined both their marriages. Neither of them were employed there very long after that. I had quit by the time all this had come out.

While I was pregnant with my second son, Clark, some friends of mine came to see me at Fred Meyer. I was working and they were talking to me about selling their business to a guy who ran it into the ground, and then they had to take it back from him. They wanted to sell it, and Steve wanted to buy a business of his own. I talked to Steve about it, and we eventually bought the trophy shop business called Valley Trophy.

We had the shop for about nine years. It did have its ups and downs. When I stopped working at Fred Meyer, I went to work at the trophy shop, helping Steve out as much as possible, getting the business organized.

When I had Clark, I stayed home for a while, until I needed to get back to work and bring in some more money. That meant both kids needed to be in day care. This is very expensive! Steve told me about someone who had come into the store, looking for advertising and for people to help with sales for a new phone book. He told her about me and set up an interview for me to meet with her. I had a job that night. I started on Monday, the next week. It was a great product they were selling and I made good money, but I later found out that the management wasn't the best. I had been involved in some car accidents while on the job. The company wouldn't back me like they should have. None of them were even my fault. It cost me a lot in the end. My boss lied to me a few times as well. I started to lose interest in the company, but I still needed the money. I started looking for a different job.

I prayed that something would show up where I could make the same type of money without the stress. I had three different job opportunities come my way. I knew they were good ones, but couldn't bring myself to trust that they were right for me. Each time I passed on an opportunity, I would get into a car accident soon after. It seemed as though I had become a magnet for every bad driver out there. I was continually rear-ended. The accidents steadily got worse each time until I finally realized I wasn't supposed to be doing that job anymore. It was a wake up call to me. I eventually left this company, after three years. I realized that if I had listened to the other opportunities, I would have been in a much better position. Keynote here, if you pray for God to help you, and an opportunity shows itself to you, look into it before you just blow it off and tell God it's not what you're looking for.

We tried to expand the business at the trophy shop by purchasing an embroidery machine. I was the only person to use the machine. I went for training in California for four days. When I came back, four other new embroidery shops had opened. There was a business above us that use to get their items from Anchorage. When they saw that we were doing it now, they asked me to do some coats and shirts for them. That worked out well and I was less expensive for them. That really helped me for a while. Eventually, the head manager of the business upstairs was going to retire and that office was shutting down and relocating back to Anchorage, where the next head of that department lived.

Again, I was back to needing more money. I eventually started looking for work again and found a job with a magazine production company. I was working in the Valley, trying to make their local *Military Relocation Guide* bigger and better. During this time, my previous employer at the chiropractic clinic had contacted me. They were hiring and were wondering if I was available. I told them that I was currently working, but after this assignment I didn't know what they had next for me. I didn't want to drive back and forth to Anchorage though; I did know that much. The clinic said they would wait to hire, if I was interested in the position, after I finished the job I was currently doing. I was supposed to be done with it in three weeks.

I had been in a few car accidents over the years and the doctor didn't want me out on the road anymore. It seems bad drivers had decided to use me as a target, over the years. I had nine concussions at this point in my life. Dr. Martin said I was like a professional football player who couldn't play anymore due to head injuries. If I got into another accident with another head injury, it could kill me. This helped me decide on the job I would be taking.

When I finished the ads in the magazine, it had gotten larger and I was given a nice-size bonus. The company didn't want to lose me, but

I had to think about my family and my future. I went back to work at the clinic.

When I started back at the clinic, there were plenty of people I had known before still being seen there. It was almost like a homecoming. I started back in April 2008, being glad I didn't have to drive around anymore with the gas prices going up so fast. It was pretty easy to get back into the swing of things. It didn't take much to get back to where I was before, in the learning process. Soon after, we hit the recession that took out the stock market. I remember a lot of people losing a lot of money during this time.

CHAPTER 18

The Kids

Ryan Hanlon with my family in 2007

My kids are a very big part of my life. I should give a little background on them. Our oldest is Alex. He is now fourteen years old and very smart. He's almost as tall as me now and loves to play sports. He's extremely competitive and is one of the best bowlers in the state of Alaska for his age, and has never had any real training. He just watches and learns. I don't know how he's able to teach himself and to progress as fast as he does each year, but we encourage him as long as he's interested in the sport. His other love is baseball. He's a very strong pitcher as well. He has a natural curve to his pitch that most pitchers would love to have. I love to watch him play. The other thing that he is really good at, is stealing bases. He has even stolen home plate before. He's such a competitor, that he gets upset with himself easily if he doesn't do as well as he thinks he should. I believe that with time and patience, he will do very well with whatever sport he decides to play in. He has already saved money for college in a United States Bowling Congress account. They have tournaments that he bowls in, as well as Pepsi-sponsored tournaments that allow him to earn money for college, wherever he decides to go.

Alex is also a very good student. We have taught him a good way of doing his homework so that when he decides to go to college, he can pick which one he wants to attend or hopefully even get a full scholarship. He's very good in math and loves to create things, especially with Legos. It's been his thing since he was very small. I'm very proud of him.

Alex got his name back when Steve and I were first dating and my friend, Bruce, was getting ready to have his first child. Steve and I were in the airport when he was heading to Vegas for the first time, just talking about names of kids and we'd only been dating about two months, I think. We both liked the TV show, *Family Ties,* with Michael J. Fox. This is about the time when he was telling everyone about being diagnosed with Parkinson's disease. We both liked the name Alex or Alexander and agreed it would make a very good first name. I had been told I could use the middle name of Jason Robbe for my kids if I chose to do so. Renee was going to use his first name for one of her kids. In my head, I had chosen Alexander Keith to be my firstborn's name, if I had a boy. Later on when he came around, Steve agreed on it as well.

Clark is my little comedian. He's twelve now and way bigger than his brother was, at the same age. His name was initially supposed to be Steven James, but we weren't sure if we wanted to have two Steves in the house. There is also an Uncle Steve in the Manning side of the family as well. It was too confusing. One evening we were watching TV and *Smallville* was on. It was our favorite show to watch as a family for ten years. It was a show about Clark Kent, aka *Superman*, growing up in his hometown of *Smallville*. I was at the kitchen table and Steve was on the couch.

He asked me, "Do you really think we should name him Steve?"

"I don't know. I think it's going to be very confusing with you being Steve and having an Uncle Steve. We can't even call him Stevie because that's what everyone who's known you forever calls you." There was a long silence. "What other names do we like that aren't being super-used right now? I don't want him being in school with five other kids having the same name."

The show came back from the commercial. Steve said, "What about Clark? I don't know any of them around here. Do you?"

"No, I must say that's not a common name right now. Did you just pull that off the show?"

"Yeah, we could name him Clark Kent; that would be cool," he said with a smile.

As I sat listening to the show and contemplating on the new name, I decided that it wouldn't be too bad. "Hmm.... Well, you can't really give a person with the name Clark Kent a bad time in school, now can you? I kind of like that idea."

"I was just kidding. Are you seriously thinking of giving him that name?"

"Why not? It's a strong name, he more than likely won't get picked on, and I do like Tom Welling. He'd be getting his name from him," I said. Tom Welling played Clark Kent in *Smallville*.

"You do realize that if we call him Clark Kent he's going to have a brother named Alexander. You know... Lex for short." We looked at each other almost laughing, but just smiling.

"It's settled then. His name will now be Clark Kent Manning. Everyone is going to get such a kick out of that one." I smiled really big. I just loved it. "We have been calling his brother Alex for so long, that we will just leave it that way."

When I went to the hospital and had Clark, the nurse wanted to know what name to write on the paper. I told her, "Clark Kent Manning." She just laughed and said, "You're kidding, right?"

I told her, "No, I'm not kidding. That's what we decided on and that's what it needs to say."

She said, "I'm not writing that. Tell you what, I'll just leave the paper on the table here and when you're ready with the name, let me know and I'll be back." She left the room.

"Fine." I said. After she left the room, I walked over to the table and picked up the paper and wrote the name on the paper myself. It was done and in ink. She couldn't believe it, when she came back in. I just laughed.

Clark is a much more emotional child than Alex was. He started out doing okay, but wouldn't sleep unless the TV was on. If I shut it off, he'd wake up crying until it got turned back on. Clark wasn't a happy child for several years. I still don't know why; he was always so mad. He didn't like day care and I had to work. It was very hard on him. It stayed this way, until he was almost in school, when he turned five. Then one day, it was like a light switch and he was a completely different child. I pray that he never changes back to the way he was. He has been a very happy-go-lucky child ever since. He's a great comedian and loves to make people laugh. He doesn't even have to try. He loves to watch *Justin Timberlake* on the *SNL* skits. He has a great memory and can tell a one-liner joke, with perfect timing.

In the spring of 2013, he took an acting class with Seattle Talent Agency and was able to go all the way through the audition process. He was even picked to be one of the kids to go through on a fast track to Hollywood program for acting and modeling. We really knew he could do well with it, but we didn't have the financial backing to get him on that track. It was his first time doing any acting and he thought it was okay. He said, "Maybe, I should take the slower road and learn a few things first. Make sure this is what I really want to do, before you spend all that money."

We thought, "Wow!" He's only ten and he can come up with that all on his own. That's a good way of thinking. We agreed with him, of course. Later that summer, the local theater was putting on a summer camp, and Clark went. He enjoyed himself and looked like he had a great time with the play called *The Granny Awards*.

He may still be young, and have a lot to learn, but I still think he would do well, if he can get into theater, a choir, or a band. He loves music and he can also dance. I think I'm going to have one really good athlete and the other is going to be some sort of an entertainer. Whatever they decide to do in life, they have our support.

CHAPTER 19

Proper Binge

I n 2009, I was working on a Thursday at the chiropractic clinic and there was a faint discussion I was hearing at the front desk, while I was cleaning a room.

My coworker walked into the room I was in and said, "Chery, there are a couple of men here who want to talk with the office manager, but I think you should talk with them as well, since it's right up your alley."

I didn't know what to say, since I wasn't the office manager or the decision maker. I walked out to the front desk and saw the two men standing in the lobby.

"This is the woman I was telling you about. Her name is Chery. She might be able to help you with what you're looking for," she said.

"I'm not the office manager though. What can I help you both with?" I asked.

They introduced themselves as Dean Q. Mitchell and Michael Burns. They started to talk about how they were local independent filmmakers and they had written a movie that they wanted to make in Wasilla, and were looking for businesses to help sponsor the movie.

Now, I knew why I had been brought into this conversation. "The office manager is the one you need to talk to about funds for the movie, but I can help you with a lot more than that. You both have no idea who you just came across with this information, do you?" I asked, knowing they didn't have a clue. They looked at each other. I don't think they knew if they were in trouble or not.

"I've been wanting my whole life to get into the movie business, behind-the-scenes or whatever. If you need help, I may be able to assist you."

"We're looking for people to help us raise money for the movie. We obviously don't have the sales skills needed for going to businesses and asking for money. I'm sure you can tell with how we started pitching it to you," replied Michael.

Dean said, "We do have the know-how to film, direct, and write the movies, just no real business background." They both just stood in front of me with blank looks on their faces.

"Well, I have a history of sales. I can help you get some of the money and get this underway. Do you have a script? What is the movie about?" I asked.

Michael said, "It's called *Proper Binge* and it's about a thirty-two-year-old binge drinker who still lives at home with his mom. His friends are also binge drinkers and they get into some really bad situations. The main character has a stepsister who he used to date, before their parents got married. Now the main character ends up in jail and has to go to a rehabilitation class. He's instructed to apologize to everyone he's wronged, and have it recorded on video while he's doing it. He recruits his friend's brother, who is good with cameras to help him out. Along the way, he meets up with a drunk who lives behind a bar and is shown what his life will be like if he doesn't change his ways. It's something that we both came up with, based on personal experiences, but it's not a documentary. We came up with it after watching *The Hangover*. We wanted to show a more serious side to alcoholism with a little bit of comedy to go with it." They both just stared at me, not knowing what kind of a reaction they were going to get.

"Count me in. I don't have a lot of spare time, but I will do whatever I can to help get this movie underway. I would like to see a copy of the script though," I said. I was curious how this was going to be portrayed and needed to know what information was going to be in the movie so I could have a better idea of who and where to go for help. "I've always wanted to do a movie, at least help out or something, and this gives me that chance." I smiled.

We exchanged phone numbers and they went on their way. I was so excited. This is what I had always wanted to do. I felt like I was being given the chance I thought I'd never have.

After a few days had passed, I met up with Michael and we began to talk more about who and how to approach business owners for investment opportunities. I finally got a copy of the script and began to read it. I was shocked at the language that was going to be used. I started to wonder if this is what I should really do. I had a talk with Dean. I was told that the language had already been cut down, previous to me seeing it. Since I didn't write the movie, I didn't really have any say in the matter. They explained it needed to have the language in it to be realistic. After some thought, I had to agree with them.

I prayed about the whole thing, wondering if I should do something different. Then one day in church, I got a revealing assurance that it was going to be okay. I would get the movie done, but it would be in the time frame that God had planned and we just had to be patient. It was going to be used for a much higher purpose. I was unaware what this meant and how it was going to be used for me until much later. When this was revealed to me, I broke down in tears. I knew that I was going to be used for something that just had to be made. I still felt uncomfortable about the language.

One of the places Michael and I went to was a car shop that installed Breathalyzer ignitions. I thought they would be a great company to work for us to work with. I got the phone number from the business owner for the main office in Texas, where I would need to set up a time to discuss the proposal. I was able to get the company to help us out with the very beginning of filming, after telling them my story and wishing they would have had this back then. It could have stopped the accident from even happening. The family could have had it installed in their truck as a preventative measure, so he couldn't drive drunk. Being that the court is the one who usually initiates the installment of the product, the company had never thought of using it in that way. I thought it would be a great idea for those families who have known drinkers in their households and don't want them to drive their cars. We got underway with filming that summer.

It took all summer to film, due to schedules and work responsibilities. We had a great company called The Rib Shack that donated food to us all summer while we filmed. They will never be forgotten for their help with the movie. We didn't have a lot of luck finding much funding to help us, but we found a lot of people who were willing to back us and donate whatever they could, so that we could get this movie shot. It was all those special people out there who allowed it to actually happen. Steve took on the role of tracking all the funds on the computer for tax purposes. The movie is still in postproduction, but has been submitted to The Sundance Film Festival, where I think we stand a good chance at having it looked at and taken a little more seriously. It was looked at, and there were over 12,000 submissions entered and only 310 were kept. We were told they liked the story, but had others that were better. They wished us luck and to try again with another festival.

Since filming with this wonderful bunch of people, I met more wonderful people in the same field. There's so much talent in Alaska that has been untouched. It would be great to have even a small studio in the Valley where I live, to be able to help with productions. Who knows, maybe someday it will happen. We have such a diverse climate and landscape in our state. People don't realize how much can be filmed here. It's the politics that always seem to get in the way.

CHAPTER 20

In Conclusion

W hat I have learned from my life so far, is that nothing should be taken for granted. You never know how short your life is or how it will end. Just when you think you've got everything figured out, life will change in a second. The life you thought you might have can be changed to one you never could have imagined. There are so many things I think I know, but may never truly know or find out.

There has been so many times in my life that I may have taken a different road, if I would have just made a different decision. I occasionally hear this little voice, like most of us have, telling me whether or not I should do something. Most of us call it a conscience. I call it, my voice from God. There are opportunities out there that we can have or not have, if we just listen to what we're being told. We will know deep down, if it's right or not. If you pray for something or about something, just believe in it and then step back, watch, and wait to see what happens. I have been amazed at some of the direct answers I have been given, when I least expected it. Don't have a closed mind to who's out there waiting to help. I have what I call, my auto angels, on patrol with me to keep me safe these days. I'm still here, after all that I've been through; that's got to say something.

Over the years, I have had dreams when sleeping. Everyone does, I know, but these dreams sometimes come true. They have, ever since I was a teenager. I never know which ones are going to be real or not, but recently some very memorable dreams I've been having, are coming true. Because of the relationship I have with God, I think that I'm being shown some of what's going to be happening in the near future. I've already had some disturbing dreams that didn't make any sense to me. "A war without a war." What does that mean? It was when I saw the chemical reaction on the civilians in Syria that I understood what my dream was about. It was the exact scene I dreamed that I was watching on TV playing out in front of me. It continues to happen to me today. I used to write my English papers about the dreams I would have. After my accident, I didn't have dreams for years. They eventually started coming back again and now are very realistic in nature.

I have recently read a book called *The Harbinger* by Jonathan Kahn. It was my eye-opener to what I think I need to do. Over the years, many people commented on how my story needed to be told. That way, some people who need hope can get it, see how things can happen, and maybe even find out why later. I had no idea why I was still here; it was to help people who'd been through something like this. By working at the chiropractic clinic I can also help them with getting through their car accidents. I have been trained for this my whole life without even realizing it. I always did well in school writing stories, and then eventually got my writing degree, and now I'm writing a book about miracles that happen every day. I really would love to turn this into a movie someday.

In the last twenty-five years since this accident happened, I've had my eyes opened to so many things. Never would I have imagined that I would be writing a story such as this. When all of the bad things happen in our lives, we don't know what the future outcome will be or who will be affected by it. Looking back at all the people whom I have come in contact with, one way or another, I can see how different life experiences have an effect on those around us. Some examples of these are:

The party I threw for everyone before I left for Alaska and the pilots of the helicopter who showed up and told me that no one has ever thanked them for what they do. I couldn't believe that.

Then there's the phone call I received from the one man in the group, who was the first to come to my aid, and the experience of knowing what they felt at the scene of the accident, and the miracle of the helicopter being in the right place at the right time.

Finding out one year later that Chris had talked with Jason's spirit just before she died in the hospital. He was waiting for his sister to help him with something on the other side that no one will ever know.

Some people may not believe in God or life after death. I have to say that with as much as I've been through in the forty-four years I've been here so far, I would never deny that God exists. I have felt his presence myself, and I know I want that again. I just wish that everyone could know what I know, but that's not how it works either. I will pray for this knowledge to be shown to everyone. Hopefully, in some way you will get to see things as I have. Remember, God has a reason for everything. It may not be today or tomorrow for you to be able to understand it, but you will in due time. I did, and I still do. I have watched the saying "What comes around goes around" play out many times so far. It's not always nice to see and sometimes it happens when we don't see it at all. Be mindful to what is around you. Life is too short to do things that just don't matter. Make your life matter.

There are still so many things that I want to do in life, but I don't know if they will happen or not. My responsibilities are at home with my kids and my husband right now. The one dream I've always had is to meet George Lucas and go through Skywalker Ranch. I've had different dreams at times, like wanting to meet Tom Cruise, Steven Spielberg, James Cameron, and Tom Welling. Well, the whole *Smallville* cast. I have reasons for all of them, like we all do, but George Lucas has always been the one person on this earth that I've wanted to meet and hope to be friends with. I hope one day to make that happen. I dare anyone to tell me that I can't do it. Then sit back and watch me. With God's help and patience, I believe that I can, in time.

Until then, I will continue to raise my two wonderful boys and be the best wife and person I can be. There's so much uncertainty in life right now. I think everyone is looking for some hope and curious about which direction to go. All I know is, God does exist and He is good. He saved me so that I could be here today, to write this message of hope and document the miracles that have happened to me. Life isn't forever, and we all know this. Be sure you know what you believe and with whom you'd like to spend the rest of your eternity with. I know a lot of people who have passed away. I want to see them all again. Some I know I will, and some I know I won't. If you want to feel what utter peace is like, pray to God, and only He can be the one to show you that. This life is but a journey of ups and downs. It's the experiences and people you meet along the way, that make it so interesting.

Recently, I learned through Renee Robbe that Jason's funeral was quite amazing. She said people came from all over to attend the funeral, mostly between California and Michigan. They had to make the viewing of his body two days long because so many people came to see him. There were lines of people outside the door of the church waiting to pay respects to him and his family. Renee said you'd have thought that he was a celebrity who passed away with how many people came. He made such an impression on so many people. The song that was played at the funeral was "Forever Young" by Rod Stewart. It was very appropriate since he was only twenty-two years old. Every time I hear this song, I get chills and always think that he's with me. The song always seems to come on the radio, right when I need it the most. It was amazing to find out this information twenty-five years later as I was doing research for this book. I knew about the song much earlier than this, but I had no idea the impact he made during his life.

Renee also told me that the same day I had my experience in my hospital room, the same thing happened to her in her brother's bedroom. She was crying and going through the "what if's" and "why's" of the situation when she felt a big hug. She believes it was her brother.

Renee also had reminded me of a situation when we went back to Prescott, Arizona, and I was riding with her in her new car. She had a white Prelude just like Jason's, but newer. We were heading down the mountain on a one-lane gravel road when her front wheels somehow locked up and we began to spin around several times before the rear end of the car was nearly hanging off the cliff. Just then, Renee looked down to see Jason's picture on her key chain and she heard him say, "Punch it!" She did and we made it back onto the road like nothing had ever happened. We made it safely down the mountain and never had another issue with the car.

Considering the events that have recently happened in order for me to get this book published who knows, there may be a second book of miracles for me to write about just around the corner.

I'm waiting to see what God has in store for me next. Oh, the anticipation!

About the Author

My name is Cherylyn Kay Manning. My friends and family just call me Chery. I was born on Elmendorf AFB in Anchorage, Alaska as Cherylyn Schultz in 1970. My dad was a meteorologist in the Air Force and married my mom after high school. Yes, I was a military BRAT. My older sister Dawn was also born in Alaska, in 1969. We moved around a lot when I was young. It was hard to make friends when I was little. It was even harder to keep up with them after moving or when they moved to a different location. After moving from Anchorage in 1972, we went to Hampton, Virginia, where my little sister Wendy was born in 1973. Then, we moved to Rantoul, Illinois in 1976 and after to Fort Worth, Texas in 1977, back to Illinois and finally to Duluth, Minnesota in 1978. I think BRAT means, Being Relocated All the Time.

My parents got divorced when I was ten and most of my mom's family lived in Alaska, so we moved back in 1980, permanently. We initially lived in Anchorage, for the first three years, before moving to the valley in 1983. I finished school at Wasilla High School in 1988.

I have been told for many years that this story should be written. I put it off for many years, not really understanding why I didn't just write it at the time. I know now; it was never completely ready until this point to get the entire message out. I am still learning things daily about how God works in our lives. I may even start my next book on the process of how this book got underway.

I believe, I was destined to write this book. People along my path of growing up, always made me promise to keep writing. It may have been just to a friend who was in a remote area who needed contact with the outside world or someone who gave me a journal and told me to write something in it every day. These friends helped me continue to stay on the path I needed to be, even when I didn't want to do it anymore because it seemed like a waste of my time.

There are also more stories to tell of things that happened as I grew up: the summer in high school we had no electricity and had to carry water to the house; and taking showers at the Laundromat and staying late at night to wash our clothes there. Then there was the summer my mother's car was struck, front to back, by a fallen tree in the middle of my step-uncle's driveway. Then I was almost bitten by a cottonmouth snake at the age of three in Virginia. There are so many stories to tell. Most people I know have a great story or two that can be a lot of fun to hear. Hopefully, between work, kids in school, afterschool activities, homework, weekend sports, housecleaning, and a busy personal life, I can get a few more of these stories out to the public for some entertainment and fun reading. However, there is usually a lesson to be learned with each one of these incidents. For whatever reason, it seems as though most of the major things that have happened to me have always been on Thanksgiving weekend. I find this to be very strange.